Coin Collecting for Beginners Handbook

A Simple Up-To-Date Guide to Identify, Store, & Preserve Valuable Coins, So You Can Avoid Scams & Turn Your New Passion Into Profits

Collector's Gateway

© Copyright Collector's Gateway 2024 - All rights reserved.

The content within this book may not be reproduced, duplicated, or transmitted without direct written permission from the author or the publisher.

Under no circumstances will any blame or legal responsibility be held against the publisher or author for any damages, reparation, or monetary loss due to the information contained within this book. Either directly or indirectly. You are responsible for your own choices, actions, and results.

Legal Notice:

This book is copyright-protected. This book is only for personal use. You cannot amend, distribute, sell, use, quote, or paraphrase any part of this book's content without the author's or publisher's consent.

Disclaimer Notice:

Please note the information contained within this document is for educational and entertainment purposes only. All effort has been expended to present accurate, up-to-date, reliable, and complete information. No warranties of any kind are declared or implied. Readers acknowledge that the author does not render legal, financial, medical, or professional advice. The content within this book has been derived from various sources. Please consult a licensed professional before attempting any techniques outlined in this book.

By reading this document, the reader agrees that under no circumstances is the author responsible for any losses, direct or indirect, which are incurred as a result of the use of the information contained within this document, including, but not limited to, — errors, omissions, or inaccuracies.

All rights reserved. No part of this publication may be reproduced, stored, or transmitted in any form or by any means, electronic, mechanical, photocopying, recording, scanning, or otherwise, without written permission from the publisher. It is illegal to copy this book, post it to a website, or distribute it by any other means without permission from the publisher or author except as permitted by U.S. copyright law. Collector's Gateway asserts the moral right to be identified as the author of this work.

Collector's Gateway has no responsibility for the persistence or accuracy of URLs for external or third-party internet websites referred to in this publication. It does not guarantee that any content on such websites is, or will remain, accurate or appropriate.

Designations used by companies to distinguish their products are often claimed as trademarks. All brand names and product names used in this book and on its cover are trade names, service marks, trademarks, and registered trademarks of their respective owners. The publishers and the book are not associated with any product or vendor mentioned in this book. None of the companies referenced within the book have endorsed the book.

First edition

Contents

1. Introduction — 1
2. Introduction to Coin Collecting — 4
3. Identifying Valuable Coins — 11
4. Coin Grading and Valuation — 19
5. Storage and Preservation — 30
6. Handling and Maintenance — 38
7. Budgeting and Planning — 44
8. Buying and Selling Coins — 53
9. Specialized Collecting — 62
10. The Collector's Mindset — 71
11. Navigating the Digital World — 78
12. Investing in Coins — 87
13. Expanding Your Numismatic Knowledge — 97
14. Conclusion — 106
15. References — 108

Introduction

the complexities of coin grades and mint marks and the fear of falling for scams. But driven by a genuine fascination and aided by seasoned collectors, I slowly upgraded my casual interest into expertise and a profitable hobby. I'm eager to share my knowledge and simplify this process, ensuring your path is much smoother.

This book explains the layers of coin collecting, making it accessible and straightforward for beginners. You'll learn to identify valuable coins, understand the best practices for storing and preserving your collection, and navigate the buying and selling aspects of the hobby without falling prey to common pitfalls and scams. By combining practical advice with the latest market insights, this guide ensures you're well-prepared to make intelligent, profitable decisions.

I packed this book with tips and detailed, step-by-step instructions that cater to your foundational needs and the nuances experienced collectors will appreciate. From budgeting for your first purchases to exploring advanced collector strategies, each chapter builds on the last, creating a thorough roadmap that adapts to your growing skills.

What sets this book apart is its commitment to keeping you in the know. Staying current is vital in coin collecting, as market values can swing dramatically. That's why I've prioritized providing the most up-to-date information available, equipping you with the knowledge to act swiftly and confidently. But this book isn't just about relaying facts; it's about sharing stories from collectors, showcasing studies, and offering insights into numismatics's historical and economic contexts.

The approach here is straightforward and friendly. Please consider this book a conversation with a knowledgeable friend who is excited to share all the tips and tricks they've learned. Whether you're sorting through your first coins or are ready to invest in pricier pieces, the guidance here remains clear and relatable.

This book is structured to walk you through every aspect of coin collecting, from the basics to more advanced practices like digital numismatics.

With this book in hand, you're a reader and fellow explorer stepping into a realm rich with history and opportunity. Let's uncover the mysteries of coin collecting together and turn what may begin as a hobby into a rewarding journey of discovery and profit.

Introduction to Coin Collecting

Did you know the first coins were minted around 600 BCE in Lydia, now part of modern Turkey? These ancient coins weren't just currency but miniature masterpieces of art and symbols of the empires that produced them. Today, each coin you encounter, whether tucked away in an old attic box or handed to you as change from a morning coffee, carries a piece of history, a piece of an economic puzzle, and a story waiting to be told. This chapter will take you through the captivating world of numismatics, helping you understand the value, joy, and enrichment that coin collecting can offer your life.

The Fascinating World of Numismatics: A Brief Overview

Numismatics is the study and collection of currency, including coins, tokens, paper money, and related objects. The practice goes beyond a collection; it explores the socio-economic, political, and artistic landscapes of various cultures and eras. Coins are like time capsules, each with the stories of the past—tales of inflation, fallen empires, public triumphs, and personal memories. When you hold a coin, you are holding a piece of history passed through countless hands, each leaving a mark on its journey through time.

Coin collecting is a diverse hobby, appealing to people of all ages and from all walks of life. It can range from collecting readily available coins from current circulation to acquiring rare and ancient ones requiring more significant investment. Some collectors focus on coins from specific countries or historical periods, while others might be intrigued by error coins—those with mint mistakes that often turn them into collectors' items. Then, some collect commemorative coins—special issues that mark significant events or honor notable figures and milestones. No matter the focus, each collection tells a personal story, reflecting the collector's interests and passions.

The benefits of coin collecting are many. Educationally, it is profoundly enriching. As a collector, you delve into the details of historical events, economic conditions, and cultural elements that influence coin design and production. Financially, while not every collector turns a profit, many find it a rewarding way to invest. Coins, especially rare ones, can appreciate over time. Recreationally, coin collecting offers a fulfilling and relaxing escape from the everyday hustle. It's a hobby that can be pursued alone or with others, fostering a sense of community among like-minded enthusiasts. Collectors often share their knowledge and treasures with others, finding joy in exchanging information and appreciation.

If you're new to this hobby, the first step is to educate yourself. Begin by visiting local museums or libraries, where you can find books and exhibits on coins and their histories. Joining a coin club or online forums can also provide support and deepen your understanding. These communities are invaluable for beginners, offering insights and advice from more experienced collectors. Start by collecting coins that interest you; this could be anything from your home country's current currency to more exotic and ancient coins, depending on your interests and budget. Remember, the key to a rewarding collection is patience and persistence—qualities that will serve you well on this exciting adventure.

To truly connect with the hobby, consider keeping a coin collecting journal. In it, record the coins you collect, why you chose them, and any research you've conducted about their history and value. Reflect on what each piece adds to your collection and what you've learned from acquiring it. This practice enhances your appreciation of the hobby and helps organize and maintain your collection thoughtfully.

In this initial step into the world of numismatics, you are starting on a path that is both educational and rewarding. As you grow your collection, you'll gain a deeper appreciation of history and art and develop an eye for detail and value. Whether for pleasure, investment, or both, coin collecting opens up a world of possibilities and discoveries.

Understanding Coin Grading to Start Your Collection

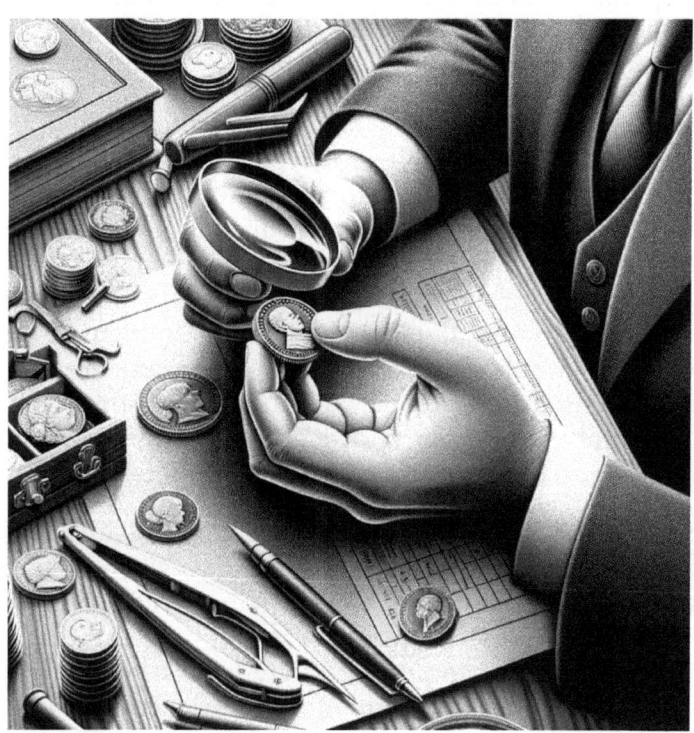

Grasping the concept of coin grading is like deciphering a map before embarking on a thrilling adventure. It's a skill that can unlock the hidden potential of your coin collection, leading you to exciting discoveries. Coin grading is a systematic process used to determine the condition of a coin. Each grade reflects a level of preservation and quality, significantly impacting a coin's overall value. The Sheldon Scale, commonly used in the United States, is a key to this understanding, with each increment potentially revealing a significant difference in a coin's market value.

The condition of a coin is critical in numismatics. It's not just about how old a coin is; it's primarily about how well it has been preserved over the years. Coins in top condition (higher grades) are typically more desirable and hold more significant value. This desirability stems from the rarity of finding older coins in such well-preserved states. Understanding grading is essential for every collector, especially if you are considering your collection as a potential investment.

Mastering coin grading can seem daunting for beginners, but numerous resources are available to ease this learning curve. Books (like this one) and websites dedicated to numismatics often provide detailed grading guidelines, complete with high-resolution images and descriptions of what to look for at each grade level. Attending local coin shows and local coin shops can offer practical learning experiences. Here, you can observe coins, ask questions, and discuss grading criteria with more experienced collectors and professionals. These interactions are invaluable; they provide insights that purely digital resources may not capture. Additionally, consider joining a numismatics club or online forums where you can post pictures of your coins and receive feedback on their conditions from experienced collectors.

When you begin grading coins yourself, start with the basics. Look at several coins in your collection and note their differences. Focus on aspects such as luster, which refers to the original shine of a coin that hasn't worn off. A coin with full luster is likely to have a higher grade. Also, examine the coin for any scratches, marks, or wear, particularly on the high points of the design. These imperfections can lower a coin's grade significantly. Practicing this discernment will enhance your grading skills, enabling you to make more informed decisions about buying and selling coins. Remember, the key to successful coin grading is patience and continuous learning;

the more you practice, the better you'll uncover the true worth of each piece in your collection. In Chapter 3, we will go into more detail on coin grading.

Mint Marks and Their Significance

Mint marks are small symbols on coins, each representing the specific mint where the coin was produced. These marks serve as a geographical footprint, providing collectors and historians valuable information about the coin's origin. Mint marks have a rich history that dates back to ancient times when mints began to leave distinctive symbols on the coins they struck. This practice helped authorities manage production and maintain quality control across various locations. In modern coin collecting, understanding, and recognizing these marks can significantly influence a coin's historical significance and market value.

The placement of mint marks can vary depending on the country and the specific minting practices of the time. In the United States, for example, common mint marks include "P" for Philadelphia, "D" for Denver, and "S" for San Francisco. To locate these marks, examine the coin carefully, typically near the date, at the bottom of the obverse (front) side, or on the reverse (back) side. Each coin's design might influence the mint mark's location, so familiarizing yourself with the layout of different coins is beneficial. For instance, on the Roosevelt dime, the mint mark is found just above the date on the obverse side, whereas on the Lincoln cent, it's located below the date.

The presence or absence of a mint mark can significantly impact the value of a coin. Certain mints are less common than others, making their coins rarer and more desirable to collectors. For example, coins struck at the Carson City mint (marked with "CC") are especially prized due to the mint's relatively short operational period and the limited number of coins it produced. Similarly, a coin without a mint mark can also indicate rarity, such as the 1909 VDB Lincoln cent from the Philadelphia Mint, which did not use a mint mark and is highly sought after by collectors.

Given the influence of mint marks on a coin's collectibility and value, some collectors focus exclusively on this aspect. Collecting by mint mark involves selecting coins based on the mint where they were produced rather than solely on their denomination or year. This approach can offer a fascinating glimpse into the history and distribution of mints and their coins. It allows collectors to build specialized collections that tell a more detailed story of numismatic history, showcasing different mints' unique attributes and rarities. For those starting, consider beginning with a specific series of coins, like the Morgan silver dollars, and aim to collect examples from each mint that produced them. This method structures your collecting efforts and deepens your understanding and appreciation of the minting process and its historical context.

Collecting coins by mint mark can be particularly rewarding, offering a clear path to follow and specific goals to achieve. It's a way to connect with the history behind each piece, understanding when and where it was used and the unique characteristics of its place of origin. As you delve deeper into this focused collecting, you'll likely discover stories of mints that have risen and fallen, shifts in economic policies, and changes in coinage technologies—all of which are etched into the small but significant mint marks on each coin.

Setting Up Your Coin Collecting Goals

When beginning coin collecting, it's vital to pause and think deeply about what draws you to this hobby. Is it the historical allure, the artistic designs, or the potential financial gain? Understanding your motivations will help you define the types of coins you want to focus on. Some collectors are captivated by the historical stories embedded in ancient coins. In contrast, others might find excitement in tracking down modern error coins that tell a story of mint mishaps. The beauty of this hobby lies in its diversity, allowing you to tailor your collection to reflect your interests and passions.

Once you have a clear idea of what fascinates you about coins, setting concrete goals can turn your initial curiosity into a structured and rewarding hobby. Start with short-term goals; these are your immediate, achievable objectives for the first year. You may aim to acquire five coins from the Roman Empire or to complete a set of circulating commemorative quarters from your country. Whatever your focus, short-term goals should be specific, measurable, and realistic. They serve as stepping stones, giving you early successes that boost your confidence and deepen your interest in the hobby.

Long-term goals are your broader aspirations that might take several years to accomplish. Maybe you dream of owning a coin from every historical era or building a collection that includes a rare coin from each continent. Long-term goals require patience and persistence, but they provide direction and a sense of purpose to your collecting efforts. They are the milestones that you will work towards over the years, offering challenges and the thrill of the chase that many collectors find irresistibly rewarding.

To effectively set and achieve these goals, creating specific strategies is essential. Budgeting is critical, especially if you are eyeing more expensive or rare coins. Determine how much you can reasonably afford to spend on your hobby each month without affecting your financial stability. Setting aside a part of your budget for unexpected opportunities is wise—a rare coin might pop up at a price you can't pass up. Alongside budgeting, thorough research is crucial. Learn as much as you can about the coins that interest you. Knowledge is power in the numismatic world—it helps you make good decisions to avoid costly mistakes. Utilize resources like books, online databases, and numismatic clubs to gather information and connect with more experienced collectors who can offer advice and support.

Remember, every collector's path is unique. Your goals might evolve as you move deeper into the hobby, and that's normal. The key is to remain flexible and open to new opportunities and directions. Your initial interest in medieval European coins might expand into a fascination with the broader historical context of the era, leading you to collect related artifacts or delve into historical research. This evolution can enrich your experience, making coin collecting a continually rewarding part of your life. As you progress, revisiting and adjusting your goals will keep your passion alive, ensuring that your collection remains a source of pride.

Identifying Valuable Coins

Imagine strolling through a bustling flea market on a sunny weekend morning. Each booth and table bursts with potential treasures, but your eyes are drawn to a small, unassuming box filled with old coins. Each coin, from the most dulled and tarnished to those that glimmer, holds a story, a piece of history you can hold. But how do you know if any are truly valuable? This chapter guides you to understanding what makes a coin exciting and potentially a valuable addition to your collection.

Understanding the Key Features of a Coin

Every coin, regardless of origin or age, shares standard features crucial for you to recognize and understand. The obverse of a coin is typically considered the "front." It often features a prominent design or portrait, which can sometimes be a clue to its value. The reverse, or "back," usually carries a national emblem or a design related to the coin's theme. The edge of the coin can be plain, reeded, lettered, or decorated, which sometimes adds to the coin's appeal and can be a security feature. Lastly, the mint mark, a small letter or symbol, usually found on the obverse or reverse, indicates where the coin was minted. Each element plays a role in the coin's identity, story, and potential worth.

The design of a coin is often a reflection of the era in which it was created. Elements such as portraits, national symbols, or commemorative motifs are artistically appealing and are markers of historical and cultural significance. Collectors often seek out coins with unique or intricate designs, as these can represent pivotal moments in history. For instance, U.S. quarters featuring different U.S. states or national parks can be more desirable due to their aesthetic appeal and educational value. The design of a coin can significantly influence its collectability and market value.

Coins are minted from various materials, adding to the overall appeal and value. Common metals include copper, nickel, silver, and gold, with precious metal coins generally being more valuable. The composition can also influence a coin's durability and appearance over time, affecting its desirability among collectors. For example, silver coins might tarnish, giving them a distinct patina that can enhance or diminish their appeal, depending on collector preferences. Understanding the materials that make up a coin helps you appreciate its aesthetic qualities, potential longevity, and value.

As you grow more accustomed to the world of numismatics, you might find yourself drawn to specific designs that resonate with your interests or aesthetic preferences. These designs can be a fun way to focus your collecting efforts. You might collect coins featuring iconic leaders, symbolic animals, or architectural wonders. Each collection can tell your story through the coins you choose to gather and treasure. This approach not only personalizes your collection but can also make your hobby even more meaningful and enjoyable.

To help you understand coin features, here's a simple exercise. Gather a few coins of different types and lay them out. Study their obverse, reverse, edges, and any mint marks. Use a magnifying glass if necessary to note the finer details. Record your observations and research any symbols or unfamiliar terms you encounter online. This practice will solidify your knowledge of coin anatomy and improve your ability to assess coins quickly and accurately.

Engaging directly with coins and their diverse features opens up a new dimension of appreciation for what might otherwise seem like simple pieces of metal. Remember that each element you study adds a layer to your understanding, making you a collector and protector of historical artifacts.

Rare Finds: How to Spot Valuable Coins in Your Change

When you are sifting through a handful of change after a day's shopping amidst the usual clutter of ordinary coins, could there be a hidden gem? It's possible, and knowing how to spot these potential treasures can turn an ordinary day into an extraordinary one. Searching for rare coins can be as thrilling as rewarding, especially when you know what to look for.

First, familiarizing yourself with what circulates in everyday transactions will boost your odds of spotting something out of the ordinary. Start by inspecting the coins you handle daily. Look for coins that seem out of place. They may be older than the rest or bear unfamiliar designs. A sudden color, size, or design difference could be your first clue to something rare. For instance, wheat pennies, which were last minted in 1958, occasionally turn up in change. Their distinctive "wheat" engraving on the reverse makes them easy to spot. Keeping a keen eye on these slight differences trains you to notice differences that could be rare or valuable.

Another helpful tip is to check the coin's date. Older coins are generally more likely to be rare, especially those minted during years of lower production. A quick online search can tell you the mintage numbers for most coins; those with lower mintages are often more valuable. Also, look for limited-edition commemorative coins. These were minted in smaller quantities for special occasions and can sometimes be found circulating with regular coins.

Beyond rarity, specific characteristics can significantly enhance a coin's value. One major factor is the coin's condition. Coins in near-mint condition are typically more valuable than those worn or damaged. Features to examine include the luster, which should be intact if the coin is uncirculated. The sharper and more defined the coin's details, the better. In a well-preserved coin, you should be able to see fine details like the strands of hair on a portrayed figure or the intricate lines in the design.

Any unusual features, such as misprints or double dies, are errors that can make a coin particularly valuable to collectors. While you might not find an error coin in your change every day, being aware of these possibilities increases your chances of recognizing one if it does appear.

Knowing a few famous rare coins can also be helpful for a beginner. The 1943 copper penny is one of the most sought-after coins by collectors. During World War II, the U.S. government made pennies from steel due to copper shortages, and a few were mistakenly struck in copper and released into circulation. Another example is the 1955 double die penny, where the date and some of the lettering were mistakenly imprinted twice. Coins like these are celebrated for their rarity and the stories they carry, making them valuable.

When you come across a coin you suspect might be valuable, handling it correctly is crucial. Always hold coins by their edges, avoiding touching the faces as much as possible to prevent oils from your skin from damaging them. If you've found something special, consider investing in a small magnifying glass or jeweler's loupe. This tool lets you look closer at the finer details and the coin's condition—more on handling coins in a later chapter.

Before making any decisions about your findings, do a bit of research. Look up the coin to understand its history, rarity, and typical market value. Websites, coin-collecting books, and online forums provide a wealth of information. Suppose the coin is particularly rare or potentially very valuable. In that case, you should consult a professional coin appraiser or numismatist who can offer a more detailed evaluation and authenticity check.

Each coin you examine could be more than just spare change. It could be a small piece of history, a work of art, or a valuable collectible. With some knowledge and curiosity, you can start discovering these hidden treasures in your everyday life, turning the act of handling change into an exciting treasure hunt.

Error Coins: Misprints That Could Be Worth a Fortune

In coin collecting, error coins hold a place of intrigue and unexpected value. Error coins are often the result of mishaps in the minting process and range from subtle misalignments to dramatic double strikes. Each error coin is a testament to numismatics' imperfect yet captivating side, where even mistakes can become treasures. Let's explore the common types of errors you might encounter, why they're so prized, and how you can start spotting and investing in these numismatic anomalies.

Understanding the various types of errors can transform how you look at every coin that passes through your hands. One common error is the double die, where a coin struck twice with a misaligned die creates a noticeable doubling effect on its designs or inscriptions. A double die can make details like the date or a president's profile appear ghostly. Another common error is the off-center strike, where the coin blank is incorrectly centered when struck. This error results in an uneven design, with one part of the coin typically having no design. Then there are the blank planchet errors, where the metal disc intended to become a coin misses the stamping process entirely yet somehow still makes it out into the world. Each error, from the dramatic to the subtle, tells a story of a moment gone awry in the mint, making them fascinating to collectors.

The allure of error coins lies not just in their uniqueness but also in their potential value. Error coins are scarce, often caught and destroyed by the mint before they reach circulation. Those that do slip through carry a piece of history, the human error aspect behind the highly mechanized minting process. Collectors value these coins based on the rarity and severity of the error. For instance, a dramatically off-center strike that features a significant part of the blank planchet can fetch a higher price than a minor misalignment. The most valuable error coins combine rarity with high demand from collectors, often driven by the peculiarity and visibility of the error.

To spot error coins, begin by examining coins you already own or encounter daily. Look closely at each piece under good lighting and consider using a magnifying glass to inspect for irregularities. Pay attention to details such as misaligned edges, double images, or design parts missing or overlapping. Coin shows and auctions are also prime places to find error coins. Dealers often have sections dedicated to these misprints, allowing you to see and compare various errors. Engaging with other collectors can provide insights into the most common errors and how to spot them. Learning from experienced collectors can help you avoid scams as well.

Considering error coins as an investment requires a good eye for detail and a deep understanding of what makes each piece unique. The market for error coins can be volatile, with values fluctuating based on collector interest and market trends. Investing in error coins can be rewarding, especially if you specialize in a particular type of error or focus on errors from a specific minting period. Building a collection of error coins offers the potential for financial gain. It brings a sense of satisfaction in owning pieces that stand out due to their stories of imperfection. As with any investment, the key is knowledge. It is vital to understand which errors are most collectible, and monitoring how their market values change over time is essential.

Embracing the anomalies found in error coins can enrich your collection and offer a unique perspective on the minting process. These coins remind us that beauty and value often lie in the unexpected and that even mistakes can have their perfect place in the collecting world. As you continue exploring, watch for those unusual pieces; they might add an extraordinary twist to your growing collection.

Historical Coins

The allure of historical coins lies not merely in their monetary value but in the rich tales they tell of the past. These coins connect to human history, each bearing testimony to the era from which it originated. For many collectors, the appeal of historical coins is rooted in the joy of holding a piece of history in their hands, an artifact crafted by ancestors whose lives shaped the modern world. These coins are also intellectual, offering a gateway into studying how people conducted commerce, trade, and cultural exchanges across history.

Identifying coins with historical significance often begins with recognizing unique designs that reflect specific historical periods. Ancient Roman coins frequently feature iconic imagery of emperors and deities, each linked to particular reigns or religious practices. Similarly, medieval coins might display heraldic symbols that tell stories of feudal allegiances and territorial disputes. To accurately identify such coins, familiarize yourself with the visual motifs and inscriptions typical of different historical periods. Consulting specialized numismatic catalogs, attending exhibitions or talks, podcasts, and even YouTube videos can enhance your ability to recognize and appreciate the historical context of these coins.

Once a coin attracts your interest, delving into its history is rewarding and enlightening. Primary research might start with deciphering inscriptions using a guide to ancient or foreign scripts. Understanding what is written on a coin can provide crucial clues about its origin, age, and the historical figures or events it commemorates. Online databases and numismatic forums can also offer insights and additional resources. Visiting or contacting museums with numismatic collections can provide access to expert knowledge and the chance to compare your coin with professionally curated specimens. A simple coin can unfold stories of distant times and places through research, turning your collection into a personal archive of historical knowledge.

Preserving historical coins is about more than maintaining financial value. It's about safeguarding heritage for future generations. Each coin is a time survivor, and as caretakers of these artifacts, collectors are responsible for ensuring their survival. Safeguarding coins involves proper handling, storage, and documenting your collection with detailed notes on each coin's provenance (history of ownership), condition, and historical significance. This preservation aids in and enhances the collection's educational value for others.

As we wrap up this exploration of historical coins, we see how each coin in your collection is not just a piece of metal but a storied artifact that offers a glimpse into the past. Through careful identification, diligent research, and meticulous preservation, you enrich your collection and contribute to the broader tapestry of human history. These coins tell stories that are important to our shared heritage, and by preserving them, you play an essential role in keeping these stories alive for future enthusiasts. The next chapter will explain the intriguing world of coin grading and valuation, where we will explore how to determine the quality and worth of your coins, further empowering you to build a collection that is as rewarding financially as it is personally.

Coin Grading and Valuation

Visualize walking through a serene art gallery of paintings spanning centuries. As you move from one masterpiece to another, you notice that each is meticulously labeled, not just with the artist's name and the work's title but also with a grade that denotes its condition and quality. This system allows everyone to understand the value of each painting at a glance. In the world of coin collecting, understanding the grade of a coin plays a similar role, providing a snapshot of its condition and value. This chapter will guide you deeper through coin grading, helping you grasp its impact on the market value of your collection and how you can develop the skills to assess your coins.

Understanding Coin Grading Systems

The Sheldon Scale was devised in 1949 by Dr. William Sheldon. This 70-point scale, which initially assessed US large cents but is now applied universally, ranges from 1 (barely identifiable) to 70 (absolute perfection). Grades under 60 are circulated coins often denoted by descriptions like Good (G), Very Good (VG), Fine (F), Very Fine (VF), and Extremely Fine (EF), with each category reflecting more preserved detail and fewer marks or wear. Coins graded from 60 to 70 are in the mint state (MS) or uncirculated, and these are often the gems that collectors treasure most. Understanding these gradations is crucial as they directly relate to a coin's desirability and market value.

For reference, see the complete modern Sheldon Scale and ratings below. The scale features the points as follows and does skip some numbers:

/ Grade / Grade Code / Description

1 / Poor / PO / Just clear enough to identify/ badly corroded.

2 / Fair / FR / Some detail is showing.

3 / About Good / AG / Has readable lettering and is heavily worn.

4 / Good / G, G4 / The coin's Rims are slightly worn, the design is visible, and there are many worn parts.

6 / Choice Good / G+, G6 / Rims of coin are complete. Peripheral lettering is full.

8 / Very Good / VG, VG8 / Some details are visible. Two to three letters of the word LIBERTY are visible, and the rims are complete.

10 / Choice Very Good / VG+, VG10 / Most designs are worn flat, and most lettering remains readable. Five to six letters of the word LIBERTY are visible.

12 / Fine / F, F12 / Half of the coin's detail is worn flat, but the lettering remains readable.

and can fetch premium prices. Compared to a coin-graded VG8, it shows considerable wear but retains full designs and lettering.

Professional grading services are invaluable for collectors looking to buy or sell valuable coins. Companies like PCGS (Professional Coin Grading Service) and NGC (Numismatic Guaranty Corporation) are respected authorities in the field. These services apply a grade using the Sheldon Scale and encapsulate coins in tamper-proof holders with a label displaying the grade. This process, known as slabbing, preserves the coin and officially documents its condition, enhancing its credibility and ability to be sold.

Professional grading services can be advantageous when you acquire a coin whose value is significantly impacted by its grade. The difference in value between an MS65 and an MS66 can be substantial, sometimes in thousands of dollars, depending on the coin. Professional grading provides peace of mind and a reliable, universally recognized assessment of a coin's condition, which is crucial when buying or selling high-value coins.

Developing your grading skills can enhance your enjoyment and efficiency in collecting, allowing you to assess potential purchases and understand the value of your coins without always needing third-party input. Start by familiarizing yourself with the grading standards. Examine coins whose grades are known (ideally professionally graded) and compare them with others to see how they differ—attention to details such as luster, strike quality, and wear locations. Over time, you'll begin to notice subtle differences that affect grading.

Understanding grading can significantly influence your collecting strategy. It can determine whether you decide to sell a coin now or hold onto it, hoping its grade appreciates over time as it becomes rarer. Moreover, when purchasing new additions, knowing the grades that offer the best balance between cost and potential appreciation can help you build a more valuable collection without overspending.

<u>To put your new knowledge into practice, try this grading exercise.</u>

1. Take three coins from your collection and attempt to grade them yourself using the Sheldon Scale and a jeweler's loupe or magnifying glass.

2. If available, Record your estimated grades and compare them to professional assessments.

3. Reflect on discrepancies and consider what factors might have contributed to different grading outcomes.

As you continue to explore the fascinating world of numismatics, remember that coin grading is both a skill and a science. It requires a sharp eye, attention to detail, and a deep appreciation of each coin's unique characteristics. By understanding and applying the principles of coin grading, you enrich your collecting experience and enhance the potential value of your numismatic endeavors.

The Value of Getting Your Coins Graded

As you delve deeper into the world of coin collecting, you'll realize that it's not just a hobby but also a significant investment. In this context, the decision to have your coins professionally graded takes on a new level of importance. Each coin is a unique story, and its actual value can only be unveiled by the discerning eye of a professional grading service. These services go beyond assigning a grade; they unlock the hidden potential of your coins, making them more marketable and often significantly increasing their value in the collector's market.

Professional grading offers many advantages. It objectively assesses each coin's condition, providing a clear, unbiased grade based on standardized criteria. Even seasoned collectors can find it challenging to remain impartial when evaluating their treasures. A professional grade offers reassurance to potential buyers about the coin's authenticity and condition, making transactions smoother and more transparent.

Professional grading enhances your collection's credibility and visual appeal. Slabbed coins are easier to store, manage, and present, making them attractive not just to collectors but also from a display perspective. They give your collection a polished, professional look that fellow collectors and non-collectors admire.

Choosing the right grading service is crucial. Established services like the NGC and PCGS are known for their stringent grading standards and consistency. When making your selection, consider their reputation in the industry and look for reviews, testimonials, and feedback from other collectors. Assessing their expertise in the specific coin categories you're interested in is also essential.

Cost is another critical consideration. Professional grading services are charged by the coin, with fees varying based on the type of coin, the level of service (standard vs. express), and any additional services like conservation or imaging that you select. Ensure the potential increase in value from grading aligns with these costs, particularly for more common or less valuable coins that might not significantly benefit from grading. I do not recommend getting low-value coins graded.

The submission process for grading your coins is straightforward but requires attention to detail. You'll need to inventory and prepare your coins for submission accurately. Grading involves filling out a submission form that details each coin's specifics, such as type, date, and notable features. Packaging your coins securely is crucial to avoid damage during transit; this involves placing each coin in a separate, soft pouch and then in a padded box. These costs need to be considered.

Once your coins reach the grading service, they undergo an initial examination to verify their eligibility for grading. They are then assessed by expert graders who evaluate the coins under controlled lighting and magnification. This process can take a few days to several weeks, depending on the grading service and submission type.

When you receive your graded coins, each slab will include the coin's grade and identifiers, such as mint marks and special features noted during the grading process. Understanding these details can help you evaluate your collection's strengths and areas where you can improve the collection. Many grading services provide online access to photographic records of graded coins, allowing you to compare your coins against others in similar grades. This knowledge empowers you to make better and more informed decisions, ensuring your collection grows in size, quality, and value.

Factors That Affect Coin Prices

The value of a coin isn't just determined by the material from which it is made. Several factors affect the monetary worth of your coin, transforming it from a simple circular disk into a valuable collector's item. Understanding these factors can significantly enhance your ability to manage and expand your collection effectively.

Market demand is a key driver of a coin's price. It's akin to a popularity contest, where the more coveted a coin is, the higher its price tends to be. Demand can be swayed by factors such as a coin's aesthetic appeal, historical significance, or rarity. Coins with intricate designs or those that commemorate significant historical events often pique more interest. Launching a new series by a mint can also spark a frenzy among collectors. Conversely, if a coin is common or lacks aesthetic and historical appeal, it may not command high prices in the market, regardless of its age or composition.

Rarity and historical value are pivotal in shaping a coin's market value. A coin's rarity is often a result of limited mintage numbers; fewer coins produced means fewer coins available, increasing each coin's rarity. However, rarity alone does not dictate value unless coupled with demand. A coin might be rare because only a few were made, but if no one is particularly interested in that issue or series, its value might not be significantly high. Yet, a coin that is both rare and highly sought after can command staggering prices on the market. A rare coin from a popular series or a famous error coin pulled from circulation can become the star of auctions, often fetching prices over its face value.

The historical importance of a coin can influence its appeal and value. Coins that have stood the test of time and carry stories from the past are often coveted items in collections. Coins minted during significant historical events or periods bring with them not just intrinsic but historical value. Some examples are those coins produced during the reign of a famous monarch or coins that have survived monumental historical events like wars or economic crises. These coins serve as tangible connections to the past, and their stories make them valuable to collectors who cherish the depth and context they add to their collections.

Understanding how these factors, market demand, rarity and availability, condition and grade, and historical significance, interact and influence the value of coins provides you with a solid foundation for making more informed decisions. These insights are invaluable whether you are buying new coins to add to your collection, assessing the potential sale value of part of your collection, or simply trying to understand the worth of your numismatic holdings. They help you appreciate the value of your coins and understand the larger picture of what makes coin collecting a unique and rewarding endeavor.

Keeping Up with Market Trends

As a passionate collector, staying informed of market shifts and trends allows you to make informed decisions and enhances your engagement with the numismatic community. Let's explore how you can effectively track market prices, understand what drives market fluctuations, and develop strategies to optimize your buying and selling timing.

The ability to track the current market prices of coins is a fundamental skill that can influence your collection's potential growth and sustainability. Numerous online platforms and tools are dedicated to providing up-to-date pricing and auction results. Websites like PCGS, CoinFacts, and NGC Coin Explorer offer comprehensive databases to view recent sales, price histories, and population reports for various coins. These platforms often include high-quality images and detailed descriptions, allowing you to compare your coins against those sold in the market.

Subscribing to price guide newsletters or magazines such as the "Greysheet" (Coin Dealer Newsletter) or the Red Book (A Guide Book of United States Coins) also provides a regular update on the shifting values. These publications are respected for their accuracy and depth. Engaging with apps that alert you to real-time price changes can help you respond more swiftly to market opportunities or threats. By setting up alerts for specific coins in your collection, you're always in the know, never missing a beat in the fast-paced trading environment.

Complex factors influence the coin market, each adding to the pricing landscape. Economic conditions play a significant role; during economic uncertainty, more collectors and investors might turn to gold and silver coins as safe havens, driving their prices. A robust economy might boost disposable incomes, allowing more individuals to indulge in collecting, thereby increasing demand and prices for historical coins.

Collector trends also significantly impact market fluctuations. Introducing a new, popular coin series can shift interest and resources away from older series, affecting their market values. Similarly, anniversaries or significant historical dates can renew interest in related thematic coins, temporarily boosting prices. By understanding these patterns and how they influence market dynamics, you can better anticipate changes and adapt your buying or selling strategies accordingly.

Mastering the art of timing in the coin market can enhance both your collection's value and your enjoyment in building it. Regular observation and patience are your most reliable tools to buy low and sell high. Keep closely monitoring market trends and upcoming events that could influence coin values. Suppose a particular coin type is about to have a significant anniversary. In that case, you might anticipate increased collector interest and higher prices, so securing such coins beforehand could be advantageous.

Also, it would help if you considered the liquidity of different coin types. Liquid coins can be bought and sold more quickly and with less impact on their market price, providing flexibility in timing your transactions. Developing relationships with reputable dealers can also offer you insider insights and priority access to sales or auctions, giving you an edge in acquiring desirable coins before they peak in price.

Staying informed is crucial for keeping up with the numismatic market. Regular participation in forums and discussions on platforms like Collectors Universe or the NGC Forums can provide firsthand insights from other collectors and professionals. These communities are often the first to spot new trends or shifts in the market, offering a diverse and valuable collective knowledge base.

Attending coin shows and auctions in person or virtually keeps you connected to the market's pulse. These events are gatherings of enthusiasts and experts where knowledge, stories, and insights are exchanged freely. Here, you can gauge the market's mood, see which coins are gaining attention, and adjust your collection strategies to align with emerging trends. We will dive deeper into coin shows and auctions in later chapters.

Incorporating these methods into your collecting routine creates growth and learning opportunities. By staying educated, connected, and strategic, you ensure that your collection not only withstands the ups and downs of market trends but thrives.

The strategies and insights discussed here provide the tools to navigate this dynamic market and ensure your collection grows in value and significance. As we turn to the next chapter, we'll explore the storage and preservation of your treasures, ensuring they continue to inspire and appreciate in value for years to come.

Storage and Preservation

The thrill of discovering a coin that tells tales of ancient kings and distant lands or one that echoes the sounds of a market from centuries ago is fantastic. Each coin in your collection is not just a piece of metal; it's a fragment of history, a bearer of stories waiting to be told and cherished. As you grow your collection, the importance of storing and preserving these treasures cannot be overstated. It's about safeguarding not just the monetary value but the historical significance and the beauty they hold. This chapter guides you through coin storage and preservation essentials, ensuring your collection remains pristine and ready to tell its stories for generations.

The Basics of Coin Storage

When storing your coins, the options are as varied as the coins themselves, each offering different levels of protection and accessibility. For most beginners, starting with simple storage solutions like coin folders and albums is advisable. These are cost-effective and provide a neat and organized way to display your collection, making it easy to view and share with others. Coin folders typically have slots for each coin, labeled by year, denomination, or other criteria based on your collection's theme.

As your collection grows, consider more robust solutions like coin boxes or trays, which can accommodate more coins and provide better protection against physical damage. These storage units are usually lined with soft materials like felt or velvet, which prevent scratches and other wear. For collectors concerned about extreme security and the long-term safety of their investments, especially with high-value or extremely rare coins, investing in a safe at your home or a safe deposit box at a bank might be the best option. These provide a secure environment and protection against environmental factors and potential theft.

Environmental hazards pose a substantial threat to the integrity of your coin collection. Factors like humidity, temperature, light, and air quality can all lead to deterioration if not appropriately managed. Excessive humidity can cause coins to tarnish or develop verdigris, a green or bluish deposit that can occur on copper, brass, or bronze coins. Consider using silica gel packs in your storage areas to absorb moisture and maintain a stable, moderate temperature to prevent any damage from thermal expansion or contraction.

Light, especially direct sunlight, can also be detrimental, causing fading and sometimes chemical reactions if coins are left exposed for prolonged periods. It's advisable to store coins in a dark place or storage unit. Regularly inspecting your coins for signs of damage and immediately adjusting their storage conditions is crucial in preserving their condition and value. The next chapter will discuss maintaining your collection and hazards.

A well-organized collection enhances your hobby's enjoyment and helps its management and preservation. Begin by categorizing your coins by era, region, or type. Organizing makes it easier to find specific coins, helps track your collection's growth, and identifies any gaps that might need filling. Labeling each section clearly can save time and prevent unnecessary handling of the coins, reducing the risk of accidental damage.

For those who enjoy sharing their collection with others, consider creating a display area in your home where select pieces are showcased safely behind glass to prevent direct handling. Rotating the display items periodically can keep the exhibit fresh and exciting without compromising the safety of the showcased pieces.

Documenting each coin in your collection is essential, not just for insurance and legacy purposes but also for personal enjoyment and record-keeping. Start by creating a detailed inventory including photographs, descriptions, and historical information of each coin. Record the date of acquisition, price paid, market value, and other details helpful for insurance or future sales.

Consider maintaining a digital record using specialized software or apps designed for collectors. These platforms help organize and catalog your collection and often offer tools for analyzing its value over time, generating reports, and even sharing your collection online with other enthusiasts.

To get started on documenting your collection, here's a simple checklist to guide you in creating an inventory:

- **Photograph each coin:** Ensure good lighting and clear resolution.

- **Describe the coin:** Note the year, denomination, mint mark, and any distinctive features.

- **Record the condition:** Include details about the coin's grade and any damage.

- **Historical significance:** Briefly note the coin's history and why it's important.

- **Acquisition details:** Document how and when you acquired the coin, including the price.

- **Storage location:** Note where each coin is stored, mainly if you use multiple storage solutions.

By maintaining thorough documentation, you ensure that your precious collection is well-preserved and appreciated fully by future generations, possibly turning into a cherished family heirloom or a valuable asset.

Coin Preservation Techniques

Preserving your coin collection is like tending a garden; it requires patience, care, and the proper techniques to ensure each piece remains vibrant and intact for years. Preserving coins can seem intricate for many beginners but can be manageable. With a few simple, practical methods, you can maintain the luster and integrity of your coins without needing professional tools or expertise. Let's explore some foundational preservation techniques you can easily apply at home.

One of the most straightforward methods to preserve your coins is to handle them correctly. Always hold coins by their edges, not the faces, to minimize your skin's contact with the coin's surface. The acids and oils in your skin can cause corrosion over time, particularly on more susceptible materials like copper or silver. When viewing or showing your coins, consider using cotton gloves, which protect from fingerprints and direct contact. Another simple yet effective preservation practice is to store your coins in individual holders. Holders like those prevent them from rubbing against each other and causing scratches or other physical damage. Soft polyethylene holders or mylar flips are excellent choices as they are inert and do not contain chemicals that could harm the coins over time.

Choosing suitable materials for coin storage is crucial in preserving your treasures. Using materials designed explicitly for coin storage is essential, as many common materials can cause damage. For instance, PVC, commonly found in some plastics, can release acid over time, creating a green slime on coins and permanently damaging their surface. Instead, opt for PVC-free plastic holders and albums. Similarly, avoid using paper envelopes or cardboard boxes that are not acid-free, as the acid can leach out and tarnish or corrode your coins. When selecting a storage container, ensure it seals tightly to keep out dust, which can be abrasive, and other environmental pollutants like smoke or fumes, accelerating tarnishing.

Creating a preservation plan is another essential step in coin care. This involves setting a routine to check and maintain your coins periodically. Depending on the size of your collection and the materials of your coins, this might mean a monthly, quarterly, or semi-annual review of each coin's condition. During these check-ups, look for any signs of damage, such as tarnishing, corrosion, or scratches—more on these inspections in the next chapter. Use a lint-free, soft cloth to clean dust or debris from the coin holders gently. Additionally, ensure that your storage area maintains a consistent, moderate temperature, as fluctuations can cause materials to expand and contract, which might warp holders or containers.

Learning from seasoned collectors can significantly elevate your preservation techniques. Engaging with a local coin club or online forums offers opportunities to witness how others care for their collections and to receive advice tailored to specific types of coins or climates. Many experienced collectors are enthusiastic about sharing their knowledge and might even showcase their setups and trusted products. Attending coin shows presents a fantastic chance to expand your collection and allows you to observe and learn advanced preservation methods firsthand. Consider subscribing to numismatic publications or attending workshops and seminars focused on coin preservation. These can offer deeper insights into the latest products and techniques in coin care, ensuring you are always armed with up-to-date information to best care for your collection.

By adopting these simple yet effective preservation methods and continually seeking knowledge from more experienced collectors, you are ensuring that each coin in your collection remains not just a piece of metal but a vibrant story preserved in time. Your commitment to these techniques will pay off in the long run, as your collection will continue to shine and hold its value.

To Clean or Not to Clean

Choosing whether to clean your coins can feel like walking a tightrope. On one side, you have the allure of a shiny, pristine coin, but on the other, there's the risk of diminishing its historical value and charm. Cleaning a coin has potential pitfalls that adversely affect its desirability and worth. This is mainly because collectors often value the original surface, or patina, which develops on a coin over the years. This patina is not just dirt or tarnish; it is a layer that forms due to the metal interacting with its environment, and it often adds character and authenticity to the coin. Removing this layer can strip away proof of the coin's age and journey, making it less attractive to serious collectors and investors. Improper cleaning techniques can cause scratches, abrasions, or chemical reactions that permanently damage the coin's surface, drastically reducing its market value.

However, there are scenarios where cleaning a coin might become necessary. For instance, if a coin is coated with substances that cause corrosion over time, such as oils or salts from human handling, it is prudent to clean it to prevent long-term damage. In such cases, the key is to do it safely. The safest method is often the gentlest one. Start by using just distilled water to rinse the coin; tap water can contain minerals that might be deposited on the coin. If water alone isn't enough, you can use a mild soap with no added scents or dyes, applying it with a soft brush like a horsehair paintbrush. It's crucial to avoid abrasive materials like toothbrushes or scouring pads; these can scratch the coin. After gently washing, the coin should be delicately dried with a soft, lint-free cloth. This method can remove harmful residues without disturbing the coin's natural state.

When your efforts might risk damaging a particularly valuable or delicate coin, it's wise to consider professional cleaning services. These services, often offered by numismatic conservation experts, use advanced techniques to minimize harm while effectively cleaning the coin. Techniques might include ultrasonic cleaning, which uses high-frequency sound waves to agitate a liquid solution, gently lifting dirt and debris from the coin without physical contact, or controlled chemical dips that can remove more stubborn contaminants. Turning to professionals can be remarkably advisable for high-value coins, coins made from exceptionally reactive metals, or coins that are part of a historically significant collection. Before choosing a professional service, it's essential to research their methods and reputation thoroughly. Asking for before and after photos of their work or seeking recommendations from other collectors can ensure their capabilities and care.

Preserving a coin's natural patina is often preferable, not just for aesthetic reasons but for authenticity. A patina is a testament to a coin's age and history; it tells a story many collectors cherish. For example, silver coins may develop a warm, gray-to-black layer known as toning, which many collectors find beautiful. Collectors consider toning to enhance a coin's appearance and desirability. Similarly, ancient bronze coins can develop a green or brown patina that protects the coin from further corrosion, making it more stable and visually appealing in the eyes of many collectors. In these cases, maintaining the patina should be a priority, as it enhances the coin's connection to its past and can add to its value, both monetarily and historically.

Advanced Storage Solutions

As your collection expands, your initial storage solutions need to be updated to meet the needs of your increasing treasury. Upgrading your storage is natural and necessary to ensure your valuable pieces' long life and safety. This progression involves moving from basic storage options to more sophisticated systems that provide better protection and organization.

Modular drawer systems explicitly made for coin storage offer an excellent upgrade. These systems often feature drawers lined with felt or velvet, tailored to house individual coins in capsules or trays that prevent movement and abrasion. Such units help keep each coin isolated and make the entire collection easily accessible, allowing you to locate and retrieve specific pieces without disturbing others. If your collection includes coins of various sizes, customizable drawer systems with adjustable compartments can be particularly beneficial, providing the flexibility to accommodate multiple coin types and sizes.

Security is an essential consideration as your collection's value grows. Enhanced security measures safeguard against theft or damage. High-end safes designed for valuables, equipped with sophisticated locking mechanisms and constructed from drill-resistant materials, offer excellent protection. For an added layer of security, adding an alarm system that alerts you to unauthorized access can provide peace of mind. Considering the placement of your safe within your home, opting for discreet, hard-to-reach locations or even built-in wall or floor safes can significantly add to your security strategy. The goal is to make it as difficult as possible for would-be thieves to locate or steal your collection.

Managing a growing coin collection can be streamlined with the help of digital tools that offer robust inventory management features. Software solutions designed for collectors can help you catalog your coins. Some platforms also provide options for generating reports and analytics, which can be invaluable for assessing the growth of your collection over time. Cloud-based options ensure that your data is backed up and accessible from anywhere, adding a layer of digital security and convenience to your collection management practices.

Navigating the nuances of advanced storage solutions and embracing digital tools to manage your growing collection are pivotal steps in your numismatic adventure. These enhancements safeguard your treasures and enrich your experience, allowing you to engage with your collection in more meaningful ways. As we close this chapter on storage and preservation, we will delve into important handling and maintenance tips for coin collecting.

Handling and Maintenance

As your coin collection grows, each piece adds value and brings responsibility. How you handle and care for your coins can significantly impact their condition, value, and longevity. Think of each coin as a delicate artifact, a piece of history that has weathered years, perhaps centuries, to find its way into your collection. This chapter equips you with advanced techniques to handle and maintain your coins, ensuring they continue to delight and provide value for many years.

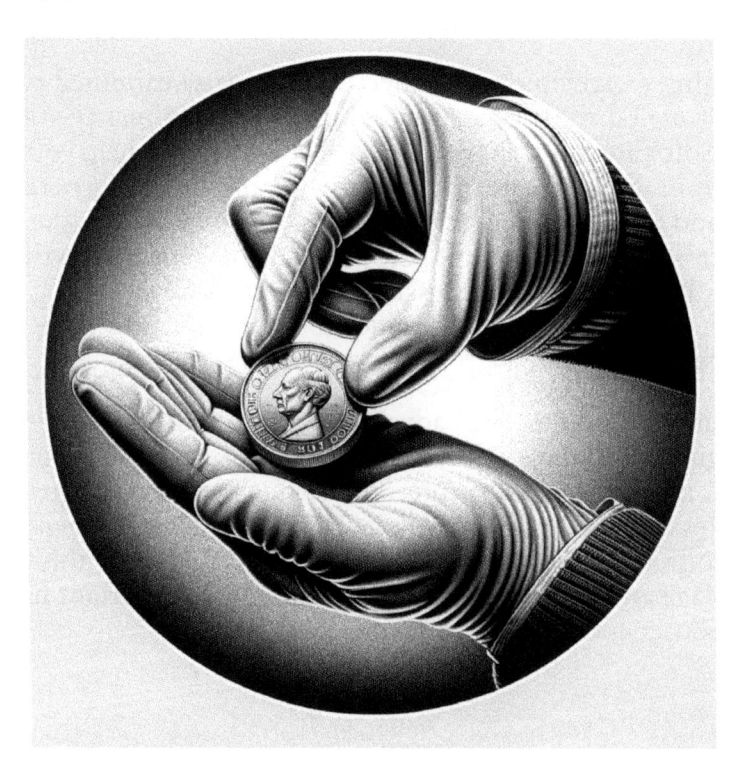

Advanced Handling Techniques for Collectors

Handling your coins correctly is the cornerstone of maintaining their pristine condition and ensuring they remain as immaculate and valuable as the day they came into your possession. Protective cotton gloves are essential when handling coins more extensively, perhaps during a detailed inspection or when displaying them to fellow enthusiasts. Cotton gloves are gentle on the coin's surface, preventing oils from your skin from making contact while providing a barrier against accidental slips or scratches. Additionally, specialized tools can enhance your handling capabilities. Coin tongs with coated tips can help you move coins without directly touching them, offering extra protection during handling. These tongs are handy when organizing or repositioning coins within your collection.

Regular inspection and care of your collection are as vital as proper handling. Establishing a routine for inspecting your coins can help you catch and minimize issues like tarnishing or environmental damage before they become severe. Set a schedule that suits your collection's size and your availability. During each inspection, examine each coin for signs of wear or damage, using a magnifying glass to get a detailed view. Check for any discoloration, spots, or signs of corrosion. This is also an ideal time to ensure that your storage solutions are holding up—that the environment remains stable and that protective holders are intact without any signs of degradation.

To aid in your regular inspections, here's a checklist to ensure thoroughness:

- Visual Inspection: Examine both sides of each coin under good lighting. Look for any changes in color, unusual spots, or signs of wear.

- Edge Check: Rotate the coin, looking closely at the edges for any dents or irregularities.

- Holder Integrity: Confirm that all coin holders are still sealing correctly and there are no signs of material breakdown.

- Environmental Check: Verify that the storage area maintains the appropriate temperature and humidity levels, adjusting as necessary.

- Documentation Review: Update your collection inventory with any changes or new observations.

This checklist can serve as a base for developing a personalized care routine that fits the specific needs of your collection.

Environmental Factors Expanded

Understanding the environmental risks to your coin collection is about preparing and protecting your valuable assets from the elements that could tarnish their beauty and diminish their value. Coins are susceptible to environmental factors such as temperature fluctuations, humidity, excessive light, and poor air quality. These elements play a significant role in preserving or damaging your coins.

Given your collection's significant monetary and historical value, the advantages of climate-controlled storage cannot be overstated. This advanced storage solution ensures a stable environment free from temperature and humidity fluctuations. Equipped with built-in humidifiers, dehumidifiers, and thermoregulation systems, these units maintain optimal conditions for your coins year-round. Particularly beneficial in regions with extreme seasonal changes or high humidity levels, climate-controlled storage provides a safe haven for your collection.

Temperature and humidity are the most important factors to monitor. Coins are made from metals that expand and contract with temperature changes. These fluctuations can cause stress and eventual wear, particularly for older, more fragile coins. Extreme temperatures can also accelerate chemical reactions that may lead to tarnishing or corrosion. Similarly, humidity can be an enemy. High humidity levels can induce oxidation, leading to corrosion.

In contrast, low humidity might dry out protective materials like paper or cardboard, making them brittle and less effective. The ideal condition for most coin collections is a stable, moderate temperature with a humidity of around 50%. Climate-controlled storage solutions, or at the very least, strategically placing dehumidifiers and air conditioners around your collection's storage area, are essential.

When it comes to environmental emergencies like floods or fires, having a well-thought-out plan is not just a good idea; it's essential. This plan should include provisions for waterproof and fireproof safes or storage containers for your most valuable or irreplaceable coins. Maintaining a digital backup of your coin inventory, complete with images and detailed descriptions, can be a saver in a disaster. Regularly updating and securely storing this information digitally or with a trusted third party is vital to your emergency preparedness plan.

For long-term storage solutions, consider the future of your collection and how best to preserve it. This might involve investing in high-quality, archival-standard storage materials that do not degrade over time. Options such as sealed capsules made from inert materials can protect individual coins from environmental factors and physical contact. For more extensive collections, tailor-made storage rooms with controlled climates and security measures might be the ultimate solution, turning your coin collecting into a legacy that stands the test of time.

Insurance for Your Collection?

Insuring your coin collection is a safety net. It might not prevent a loss, but it will certainly soften the impact, ensuring you and your collection can recover and continue. As your collection grows in size and value, the need for appropriate insurance becomes increasingly important. It's about protecting not just a financial investment but a personal passion that may have taken years to build. Understanding how to evaluate your insurance needs, choose the right policy, and ensure you have thorough documentation is essential for any valuable collection.

When you begin to assess the need for insurance, the first step is to understand the value of your collection. This isn't just about knowing what you paid for each piece; it's about understanding the current market value, which can change based on factors such as rarity, demand, and condition. Regular appraisals by a qualified numismatist or appraiser are crucial. These professionals can provide you with a detailed, up-to-date value of your collection, considering the latest market trends and sales. This appraisal should be done every few years or whenever you add a significant piece to your collection to ensure your insurance coverage meets your current needs. The appraiser can also help identify any specific risks associated with your collection that might need special consideration, such as particularly rare or fragile pieces.

Now, we are looking at choosing the right insurance policy for your collection. Typically, homeowner's insurance provides minimal coverage for collectibles and often only up to a specific value, which may be significantly lower than the actual value of your collection. Specialized collectibles insurance is more appropriate for valuable collections. These policies cover the types of risks that collections are exposed to, such as theft, damage, or loss. Some policies offer more benefits, such as coverage for damages incurred during transit or at exhibitions. When selecting a policy, consider factors such as the deductible amount, the credibility of the insurance provider, and the specifics of what is covered and what is not covered. Comparing quotes and terms from several insurers can help you find the best coverage for your needs. Feel free to ask potential insurers questions about their policies, especially how they handle claims involving collectibles, to gauge their understanding and experience.

Documenting your collection thoroughly is one of the most critical steps in the insurance process. This documentation should include detailed descriptions and high-quality photographs of each coin, receipts or proof of purchase, and records of appraisals. This information supports the value of your collection for insurance purposes and becomes invaluable in the event of a claim. Store these documents in a secure, easily accessible place, and consider keeping digital copies in a safe online storage solution. Maintaining a digital inventory that is regularly updated can streamline the process of proving ownership and value, improving the claims process if ever needed.

If the unfortunate time comes when you need to file a claim, knowing the steps and being prepared can make a significant difference. First, notify your insurance provider as soon as possible after the incident. Promptly provide them with all the relevant documentation, including any police reports, if the claim involves theft or vandalism. Be prepared to provide detailed information about the circumstances surrounding the loss or damage, and be sure to ask about the next steps and timelines for the claims process. Patience and persistence are critical during this time, as claims involving valuable collectibles can take time to resolve, often requiring detailed assessments by experts.

You place a protective barrier around your investment and passion by taking these thoughtful steps to ensure your coin collection. Insurance offers financial protection, allowing you to enjoy your collection with the assurance that it's safeguarded against unforeseen circumstances.

In wrapping up this chapter on handling and maintenance, we've explored how to care for your collection. Next, we delve into budgeting for your collection, discussing practical strategies for managing your hobby. Hence, it remains both a passion and a wise investment.

Budgeting and Planning

Imagine stepping into an old, charming bookstore. Each shelf and every corner teems with stories waiting to be told, secrets to be uncovered. Your coin collecting adventure can feel much the same, with each coin you encounter holding a fragment of history, a narrative etched in metal. Yet, navigating the numismatic world often requires thoughtful budgeting and strategic planning, especially when resources are limited. This chapter is dedicated to turning the constraints of a tight budget into a well-spring of opportunity, ensuring your passion for coin collecting grows without straining your wallet.

Starting Your Collection with a Limited Budget

Starting your coin collecting hobby doesn't need a significant initial investment. Starting small and focusing on less expensive or common coins can provide an enjoyable entry into numismatics. Consider beginning with circulated coins, often found at face value or for a minimal fee. These coins might not be rare, but they can offer valuable learning experiences. You can study their history, understand their markings, and appreciate their role in commerce and trade, all without breaking the bank.

Another strategy is to set a modest monthly or quarterly budget for your hobby. This instills discipline and allows you to plan purchases ahead of time, avoiding impulsive, potentially regrettable decisions. Focusing on the joy of collecting is crucial during this phase rather than the potential financial gain. Embrace each new addition as a step towards enriching your collection, and remember, the value of your collection isn't measured solely by its market price but also by the satisfaction and knowledge it brings.

When funds are limited, deciding which coins to add to your collection becomes critical. Prioritize coins that genuinely resonate with your interests or fill a specific gap in your collection. Suppose you're fascinated by the storied past of ancient civilizations. In that case, an affordable Roman coin might bring more personal value than a modern commemorative coin that costs the same. Always research before any purchase. This ensures that buying a coin is a well-informed decision, reducing the chances of buyer's remorse, falling for a scam, and making each acquisition meaningful.

Joining a coin club or participating in coin swaps can be a game changer for collectors on a budget. These platforms offer avenues to obtain new coins through trading, often allowing you to diversify your collection without significant expenses. Coin clubs are also invaluable sources of knowledge and networking, where you can learn from seasoned collectors and potentially receive leads on where to find deals or sales. The numismatic community is one of enthusiasts and scholars; the friendships and connections you build can be valuable, like the coins you collect.

The wealth of free resources available today can significantly improve your collection. Libraries, museums, and even online platforms offer a wealth of information. Online forums, free webinars, and websites dedicated to numismatics are beneficial for staying informed about the latest trends and market values without cost. Consider exploring online marketplaces for coins being sold at or near face value, and keep an eye out for estate sales or auctions, which can sometimes offer unexpected treasures at low prices.

As you navigate the dance of budgeting in the numismatic world, each coin you choose to collect, each decision you make, is a stepping stone towards building a valuable collection and a repository of history. The constraints of a tight budget, rather than limiting your journey, can inspire creative strategies that enhance your collecting experience, proving that the value of numismatics extends far beyond the financial. As we continue, let's explore further budgeting and financial strategies to help you effectively manage and expand your collection, ensuring your passion for collecting is sustainable, profitable, and fulfilling.

Creating a Coin-Collecting Budget

Setting a budget for your coin collecting might sound less exciting than the thrill of discovering a rare find. However, creating a budget is a fundamental step that lays the groundwork for a sustainable hobby, allowing you to enjoy your passion without financial stress. To start, evaluate your overall financial situation. How much can you realistically afford to allocate to coin collecting each month or year without compromising your other financial obligations and savings goals? This initial assessment can help you establish a budget that fits comfortably within your broader financial plan. Consider setting up a specific and separate savings account for your collecting activities. This helps manage your funds allocated explicitly for collecting and prevents you from accidentally overspending from your main accounts.

Once you've determined your spending limit, adhering to this budget is vital. One helpful method is automating your savings. Arrange a monthly transfer to your coin-collecting savings account immediately after you receive your paycheck. This 'pay yourself first' strategy ensures you consistently save for your hobby, reducing the temptation to exceed your budget. Additionally, consider using budgeting tools or apps that assist you in monitoring your spending in real time. These tools can be invaluable in helping you stay on top of your expenses, making it easier to adjust if you go over budget.

Allocating funds wisely within your coin-collecting budget necessitates balancing various expenses. While purchasing coins might be your primary focus, don't underestimate the importance of investing in proper storage and preservation tools. Also, funds should be set aside for attending coin shows or subscribing to numismatic publications, which is crucial for staying informed and connected within the collecting community. Remember, your budget should encompass all aspects of coin collecting, not just acquiring new pieces.

Saving for special purchases requires patience and discipline, especially when your eyes are on a higher-value coin or a rare find. Start by setting a specific savings goal based on the item's cost and create a timeline for when you'd like to make the purchase. Breaking your goal into smaller, monthly saving targets can make it more manageable and less daunting. If a desired coin costs $600 and you want to purchase it in a year, aim to save $50 each month. Consider setting aside unexpected windfalls, such as tax refunds or bonuses, directly into your coin-collecting fund to boost your savings. This accelerates your progress toward your special purchase and reinforces your commitment to making thoughtful, planned acquisitions rather than impulsive buys.

Monitoring your spending is critical to maintaining a healthy budget. Regularly review your spending to ensure it aligns with your budget and goals. This review should include your purchases and any costs associated with your hobby, such as travel expenses to coin shows or fees for appraisal services. If you are consistently overspending, take a step back and analyze which areas are draining your budget. Is a particular type of coin or activity causing you to exceed your limits? Understanding these patterns will help you make better, more informed decisions, ensuring your collecting activities remain enjoyable and financially sustainable.

By setting a clear budget, allocating funds wisely, saving for special purchases, and closely monitoring your spending, you create a framework that supports your passion for coin collecting. This disciplined approach ensures you can continue to grow and enjoy your collection for years while keeping your finances secure and healthy. As we continue to explore the various facets of coin collecting, remember that a well-managed budget is just as crucial as a well-curated collection, providing the stability and freedom to engage with your numismatic pursuits fully.

When to Splurge vs Save

Navigating numismatics involves making decisions that aren't just about personal interest but also about the strategic growth of your collection. As your passion for coin collecting deepens, you might find yourself at a crossroads, deciding when to save your funds and take the plunge on a higher-priced, potentially more valuable coin. Identifying the right moments to invest in significant pieces involves a blend of intuition, research, and strategic planning.

Let's talk about recognizing the right investment opportunities. Coins worth splurging on are usually those that possess rarity and have historical significance, exceptional quality, or potential for appreciation. To spot such treasures, you need to keep your knowledge sharp and up to date. Regularly engage with auction results, dealer catalogs, and numismatic publications to understand market trends and spot price anomalies that could signal a good buy. Building relationships with reputable dealers who can offer valuable insights and alert you to opportunities based on your interests and investment goals is also wise. The key is not just to acquire coins but to acquire coins that complement and enhance the value of your existing collection.

Balancing your collection is crucial as it grows. It's easy to be swayed by the allure of rare and expensive coins. Still, it's essential to consider how each addition fits within your broader collection. Think of your collection as a portfolio; diversification is vital. Allocate your budget across different types of coins to reduce risks and tap into various market segments. This might mean balancing high-cost purchases with more affordable pieces that fill historical or thematic gaps. Such an approach makes your collection more interesting and varied and spreads the financial risk across different types of assets.

When planning for big purchases, a bit of foresight can go a long way. Begin by setting clear objectives for what you want to achieve with each significant addition. Are you looking to own a cornerstone piece that will be the highlight of your collection, or are you investing in a coin that you expect to appreciate over time? Once you have a goal, set aside a dedicated savings fund for this purchase. This systematic approach disciplines your spending and builds anticipation for the acquisition, making it all the more rewarding when you finally secure that coveted piece.

Understanding the risks and rewards of significant investments is another critical puzzle. Every major purchase carries a certain amount of risk, primarily related to market fluctuations and the potential for authenticity issues. Mitigate these risks by thoroughly researching each coin before purchase, verifying its provenance, and ensuring its authenticity through third-party grading services. On the reward side, a well-considered major purchase can not only elevate the prestige of your collection. It can offer substantial financial returns if the market conditions are right. Regularly reassess your collection's value, considering market trends and historical data, to ensure your investment remains sound.

As your journey through the world of coin collecting unfolds, deciding to save or splurge is about financial capability and making strategic choices to enrich your collection's value and significance. Each decision you make shapes the future of your collection, weaving together a tapestry of history, art, and personal achievement that will stand the test of time.

Financial Planning for Collectors

As your coin collection grows in size and value, it's not just a hobby but a significant part of your financial portfolio. By implementing successful financial planning for your collections, you can ensure the growth and preservation of your investments. This brings peace of mind and prepares you for the future. Strategic purchasing, comprehensive insurance, and thoughtful estate planning are critical components of this process.

Investing in high-value coins is undoubtedly alluring. These pieces often represent the pinnacle of numismatics, being rare, historically significant, and aesthetically magnificent. However, it's crucial to approach this decision with caution and strategy. While high-value coins can be excellent financial investments, their markets can also be volatile, influenced by economic factors and collector trends. Before making a purchase, conduct thorough research or consult with experts to understand the coin's provenance, rarity, and historical price performance. Consider how this coin fits into your broader collection and investment strategy. Will it appreciate in value? Does it hold potential historical significance that could increase its desirability in the future? Answering these questions can help you make better, more informed determinations that support your long-term financial goals.

These aspects of financial planning underscore the importance of viewing your collection through financial prudence and strategic foresight. Treating your coins as valuable assets protects your financial investment and ensures that future generations can enjoy the collection, whether retained as a family heirloom or leveraged as an economic asset. As we conclude this chapter, remember that the steps you take today to safeguard your collection financially will define its legacy. The thoughtful integration of investment strategies, insurance protection, and estate planning into your collecting activities secures your collection's present and future, ensuring that your passion for numismatics leaves a lasting imprint.

In the next chapter, we'll explore the world of buying and selling coins, navigating the market, building connections, and making transactions that enhance the breadth and depth of your collection or make a profit. As you transition from collector to savvy investor, these insights will equip you to engage with confidence and expertise.

Make a Difference with Your Review

Unlock the Power of Generosity

"Coins can change your life, but sharing your knowledge can change someone else's." - Unknown.

People who give without expecting anything in return live longer, happier lives and even find more success. During our time together, I will try to make the most of this idea.

So, I have a question for you...

Would you help someone you've never met, even if you never got credit for it?

Who is this person, you ask? They are like you. Or, at least, like you used to be. Less experienced, wanting to make a difference, and needing help, but unsure where to look.

My mission is to make coin collecting accessible to everyone. Everything I do stems from that mission. And, the only way for me to accomplish that mission is by reaching...well...everyone.

This is where you come in. Most people do, in fact, judge a book by its cover (and its reviews). So here's my ask on behalf of a struggling coin collector you've never met:

Please help that coin collector by leaving this book a review.

Your gift costs no money and takes less than 60 seconds to make, but it can change a fellow coin collector's life forever. Your review could help...

To get that 'feel good' feeling and help this person for real, all you have to do is...and it takes less than 60 seconds...leave a review.

Simply scan the QR code below to leave your review:

https://www.amazon.com/review/review-your-purchases/?asin=B0D92SJ6YL

If you feel good about helping a faceless coin collector, you are my kind of person. Welcome to the club. You're one of us.

I'm that much more excited to help you identify, store, and preserve valuable coins. At the same time, you turn your new passion into profits more easily than you can imagine. You'll love the lessons I will share in the coming chapters.

Thank you from the bottom of my heart. Now, back to our regularly scheduled programming.

-Your biggest fan, Collector's Gateway

P.S. – If you provide something of value to another person, it makes you more valuable to them. If you'd like goodwill straight from another coin collector and you believe this book will help them send this book their way.

Buying and Selling Coins

Think about a bustling flea market, where every stall and corner holds potential treasures. Through the lively chatter and colorful displays, there is a glint of metal coins, each with a unique face and story. This setting isn't just a place of commerce; it's a treasure trove for collectors, offering both the thrill of discovery and the joy of negotiation. This chapter will guide you through various venues and methods for buying coins, ensuring that each addition to your collection is a wise and fulfilling acquisition.

Where to Buy Coins

The foundation of a successful coin purchase often lies in the dealer's reliability. A reputable dealer provides quality coins, ensuring transparency and trust in every transaction. To find reputable dealers, Start by seeking recommendations from fellow collectors or numismatic associations, which often have lists of vetted sellers. Attend local or national coin shows where dealers prominently display their credentials and affiliations. Look for affiliations with well-known numismatic organizations such as the American Numismatic Association (ANA) or the Professional Numismatists Guild (PNG). These affiliations are badges and commitments to ethical business practices and customer education.

When visiting a dealer, discuss your interests and ask questions about their offerings. A trustworthy dealer will be knowledgeable and willing to share information, helping you understand the nuances of each piece without pressuring you to make a purchase. They should also be transparent about the pricing, the grading standards they use, and the return policy. Before purchasing, check online reviews or Better Business Bureau ratings to see other customers' experiences. Building a relationship with a trustworthy dealer can be one of the most rewarding aspects of coin collecting, as they can become invaluable advisors and allies in your collecting journey.

Coin shows and auctions offer a vibrant environment where collectors can explore various coins, from the common to the rare. Coin shows bring together multiple dealers and collectors, providing a fantastic opportunity to compare prices, learn about different types of coins, and make informed purchases. The bustling environment can also be overwhelming. Prepare by researching the types of coins that interest you and setting a budget. Take your time to visit different booths, ask questions, and inspect coins closely. Remember, the excitement of a show can sometimes lead to hasty decisions, so it's essential to remain focused on your collecting goals and budget.

Online or in-person auctions can also be thrilling venues for acquiring coins. They often feature rare or highly sought-after items. Before participating in an auction, familiarize yourself with the process and terms, such as "buyer's premium," which is an additional fee on the winning bid. Review the auction catalog carefully, note the coins that interest you, and research their market value and history. During the auction, staying disciplined is crucial; set a maximum bid for each coin to avoid getting caught in the heat of bidding wars. Participating in auctions requires some strategy and restraint. Still, the potential to acquire a coveted piece can make it well worth the effort. In a later chapter, we will dive deeper into in-person auctions and coin shows.

You have a global marketplace where you can purchase coins from the comfort of your home. Platforms like eBay, Heritage Auctions, or specialized numismatic sites offer extensive selections. Buying coins online requires caution. Always verify the seller's reputation by reviewing feedback from previous buyers. Be wary of deals that seem too good to be true, as they often are. Request high-quality images and a video of the coin to assess its condition and authenticity before purchasing. Ensure the website offers a secure payment system and a clear return policy. Online shopping gives convenience and access to a vast inventory. It also demands vigilance to ensure the authenticity and quality of your purchases.

Joining a local coin club or society can be an enriching experience beyond buying coins, as it's about becoming part of a community that shares your passion. These clubs often have regular meetings, swap meets, and educational sessions where members can buy, sell, or trade coins in a trusted environment. They are also fantastic sources of knowledge, offering insights into the nuances of collecting, such as grading, pricing, and the latest market trends. Engaging with a coin club can provide a support network of experienced collectors who can offer advice, direct you to reputable dealers, or alert you to local buying opportunities.

As you explore the various avenues for buying coins, whether through dealers, shows, online platforms, or local clubs, remember that each purchase adds another coin to your collection and another chapter to your numismatic story. These interactions, transactions, and the knowledge you gain enrich your experience, making coin collecting a hobby and a journey of discovery. As you delve deeper into this chapter, remember that the art of buying coins is as much about the relationships you build and the knowledge you acquire as it is about the coins themselves. Each coin you choose to bring into your collection holds the potential to unlock new insights, open doors to new communities, and deepen your appreciation for this fascinating hobby.

Selling Your Coins

When the moment arrives to sell parts of your coin collection, whether to refine your collection's focus, invest in other areas, or reap the financial rewards of your collecting efforts, understanding the best practices for preparing and selling your coins can influence your experience and the outcomes. Selling your coins should be approached with as much care and strategy as you employed when acquiring them.

The first step in selling your coins is ensuring they are well-cataloged and adequately prepared. This involves organizing and documenting each piece in your collection. Start by making a detailed list of the coins you intend to sell. Record each coin's denomination, year, mint mark, grade, and unique features or historical significance. High-quality photographs are crucial, as they will be the first impression for potential buyers. Take clear, well-lit photos from multiple angles, capturing unique attributes or conditions that could affect the coin's value.

Preparing your coins also means ensuring they are in the best possible condition for sale. This doesn't necessarily mean polishing or cleaning, as often it's best to leave the patina intact; it may add to the coin's value. Instead, focus on protecting the coin from further wear. Place each coin in a protective holder with archival quality, such as a coin flip, ensuring it is secure and presented professionally. This helps maintain the coin's condition and enhances its appeal when you show it to potential buyers, giving them confidence in the quality of your collection.

Deciding where to sell your coins is a pivotal decision that can affect how much you ultimately receive for them. Each platform has its advantages and considerations. Selling through online auctions can reach a wider audience, increasing the chances of receiving higher bids for your coins. However, they typically take a percentage of the sale as a fee, and you might be responsible for shipping, which can add extra costs and responsibilities.

Selling directly to coin shops offers immediate transactions and the advantage of dealing face-to-face, allowing for more personal interaction and potentially quicker negotiations. Remember that coin shops often buy at lower prices to make a profit when reselling. Coin shows are another great venue, especially if your coins are unique or valuable. Shows allow you to interact with various dealers and collectors, potentially fetching a better price through competitive bidding right on the floor. We will dive deeper into coin shows later in the book.

Before choosing a platform, consider the specific coins you are selling and your circumstances. Auctions or shows might be the best route if you are not in a rush and have high-value coins. Local coin shops might be more practical if you need quick liquidity or have more common coins.

Pricing your coins appropriately is crucial for a successful sale. Begin by researching the current value of each coin you plan to sell. Look at recent sales of similar coins in similar conditions to gauge what buyers might be willing to pay. Resources such as price guides, online auction results, and consultations with other numismatists can provide valuable insights. When setting your prices, be realistic about the condition of your coins and how it affects their value. Setting a range rather than a fixed price can be helpful, giving you some flexibility to negotiate with potential buyers.

Emotional attachment might influence your perception of your coins' worth. While it's essential to recognize the sentimental value they hold for you, try to set prices based on objective criteria such as rarity, demand, and actual market conditions. This approach will make your prices more appealing to potential buyers and increase the probability of a sale.

Ensuring the safety of transactions, especially in online sales, is paramount. When selling coins online, use reputable platforms that offer secure payment options. Avoid accepting checks or money orders from unknown buyers, as these can be faked. Instead, secure payment methods like PayPal or direct transfers offer payment protection and transaction tracking. If you're selling in person, whether at a coin shop or a show, ensure that the transaction happens in a secure environment. Some collectors conduct high-value transactions at their bank or safe location to ensure both parties' safety.

Shipping the coins securely and with the right insurance is crucial for online sales. Use trusted shipping services that provide tracking and delivery confirmation. Invest in quality packaging materials to protect the coins during transit, ensuring they arrive at their new owner in the same condition they left you. This protects the coins and helps maintain your reputation as a reliable seller, which is invaluable if you continue trading in the numismatic community.

As you sell your coins, remember that each step, from preparation to pricing to choosing the right platform, plays an essential role in the success of your transactions. By approaching the selling process with as much care and research as you did when building your collection, you ensure that each sale reflects the actual value of your coins, rewarding your dedication.

Online Auctions and Sales Safety

As you embark on your journey into the world of coin collecting, online auctions and sales present a thrilling landscape of opportunities. With their time-bound bidding system, these digital marketplaces offer a chance to compete with fellow collectors for rare treasures. Understanding their mechanics is critical to navigating them successfully and securely. The highest bid at the close of the auction wins the coin, making the final moments a flurry of excitement. To enhance your chances of winning, it's beneficial to participate actively towards the end of the auction, a strategy known as 'sniping.' This involves placing a bid slightly higher than the current highest in the final moments, reducing the chance for others to outbid you.

Another effective strategy is setting a maximum bid limit for yourself. Most online auction platforms allow you to enter the highest amount you're willing to pay, and the system will automatically bid for you up to this limit. This keeps you within your budget and prevents the emotional bidding that can occur in the heat of the moment. However, setting a maximum bid requires thorough research. The coin's features, condition, and market values are compared by consulting trusted numismatic resources or databases. This preparation ensures that your bid is competitive yet reasonable, reflecting the coin's true value and giving you the confidence to bid.

Sellers' credibility plays a pivotal role in ensuring the security of your transactions. Start by reviewing the seller's ratings and feedback on the auction site. Look for sellers with long-standing positive reviews and those specializing in numismatics. Many reputable sellers will provide detailed descriptions and clear, high-resolution photos of the coins, offering a virtual magnifying glass to inspect your potential purchase. Feel free to ask the seller if details about the coin or its provenance need to be clarified or completed. Sellers with genuine expertise and customer focus will be more than willing to provide additional information and clarify doubts, enhancing your confidence in purchasing.

Just as when you are selling, ensure that the seller accepts secure payment methods and uses insured and trackable shipping methods. This not only safeguards your investment during transit but also provides you with a way to monitor the progress of your shipment, ensuring it reaches you safely. Request that the seller use robust, discreet packaging that does not indicate the contents' value, thereby reducing the risk of theft or damage.

Disputes occasionally arise with sellers or buyers in online transactions despite all precautions. If you find yourself in such a situation, handling it calmly and methodically is essential. Start by directly communicating with the seller to try to resolve the issue. If the dispute concerns an item's authenticity or a misrepresentation, provide clear evidence, such as photos or expert opinions, that support your claim. If direct resolution attempts fail, use the dispute resolution services offered by the auction platform or your payment provider. These services are designed to mediate between buyers and sellers and can often help reach a fair resolution. Documented and recorded communications and transactions related to the dispute can be crucial in cases where formal mediation or intervention is necessary.

Navigating online auctions and sales successfully requires a blend of strategic bidding, thorough research, and vigilant transaction practices. By understanding the mechanics of online auctions, assessing seller credibility, ensuring secure payment and shipping, and knowing how to handle disputes, arm yourself with the necessary tools to explore the expansive world of online numismatics confidently and safely.

Avoiding Scams: Red Flags Every Collector Should Know

Navigating the numismatic world can sometimes feel like walking through a maze, where every corner could unveil a discovery or, unfortunately, a hidden trap in the form of scams. As your collection grows and you become more involved in buying coins, awareness of common scams targeting coin collectors is crucial. One prevalent scam is the sale of counterfeit coins, often marketed as rare or valuable. These fakes can be convincing, particularly to those new to collecting. Another common deceit involves sellers offering coins at significantly underpriced values, which often turn out to be counterfeit or stolen. Then there are 'bait and switch' tactics, where a seller advertises a coin at a low price to attract buyers, only to claim the item is sold out and then offer a less desirable coin at a higher price.

The ability to spot red flags can save you money and the disappointment and frustration that come with being scammed. One major red flag is a deal that seems too good to be true. Proceed cautiously if a coin is sold for significantly less than its known market value. High-pressure sales tactics are another warning sign; if a seller pushes you to make a quick decision or purchase, it's often because they don't want to give you time to think or research. Be cautious of sellers who decline to provide exact information about a coin's history or provenance (history of ownership) or those who do not allow you to view the coin in person or through detailed images. Watch out for sellers who lack a physical address or use only a P.O. Box; a reputable dealer will have a verifiable physical location or a well-established online presence with transparent contact information.

Protecting yourself from scams starts with education and due diligence. Before making a purchase, take the time to research the coin and the seller. This information can help you identify inconsistencies or inaccuracies in a seller's description. Make it a habit to check the credentials and reputation of the seller, especially if they are not personally known to you. Look for reviews and check if the seller is a member of recognized numismatic organizations.

When it comes to high-value purchases, consider working with an independent third-party grading service. These services can verify the authenticity and grade of a coin before you complete the purchase, providing an extra layer of security. Always use secure payment systems that offer buyer protection, like credit cards or secure online payment systems, and avoid wire transfers or cash payments, especially with sellers you do not know well.

Unfortunately, even with the best precautions, scams can still occur. If you find yourself a victim of a scam, act quickly. Begin by contacting the seller to seek a resolution. If the seller is unresponsive or unwilling to help, escalate the issue by filing a complaint with consumer protection agencies, like the FTC (Federal Trade Commission) or a local consumer protection office. I recommend also contacting any numismatic organizations the seller claims to be affiliated with, as these groups take the integrity of their members seriously and can offer assistance or take disciplinary action.

As we close this chapter on precautions and strategies to avoid scams in coin collecting, remember that your vigilance safeguards your investments. This proactive approach ensures that each addition to your collection is a source of pride and joy rather than a cause for concern. Next, we delve into specialized collecting, exploring the rich diversity of numismatic pursuits, from thematic collections to investing in gold and silver coins, each offering unique joys and challenges.

Specialized Collecting

Thematic or topical collecting is about more than accumulating coins; it's about creating a narrative that resonates with your interests or aesthetic preferences. This approach transforms your collection into a gallery of carefully chosen pieces that reflect a specific theme, historical milestones, artistic movements, or personal milestones. Let's delve into how you can create a thematic collection that is a personally rewarding and visually compelling narrative of your chosen theme.

Focusing on History or Design

The first step in thematic collecting is selecting a theme that intrigues or inspires you. This could be anything from ancient civilizations to pivotal historical moments or even coins featuring a specific design element like ships, animals, or famous personalities. The key is choosing a theme you are passionate about, as this passion will sustain your interest and drive your efforts in expanding and curating your collection.

Some themes, like 'World War II,' offer a vast array of coins due to the global nature of the event, giving you a broad scope for collection. Others, like coins featuring a specific animal, might be more limited but can offer a deep dive into the artistic representations of that motif across different cultures and periods. Balance your interest in the theme with the availability of coins that fit the criteria, ensuring that your chosen theme is feasible for collecting.

Once you've selected a theme, the next step is to immerse yourself in research. This involves identifying the coins that fit your theme and understanding their stories. Visit numismatic libraries, attend talks and exhibitions, and connect with other collectors and experts who share your interests. Online forums and specialized numismatic sites are invaluable resources for detailed articles, catalogs, and even interactive discussions that can deepen your understanding of your theme.

Research helps you decide which coins to include in your collection. If your theme is 'The Renaissance,' understanding the historical context and the significance of different motifs used in coins during that era can help you choose pieces that are beautiful and historically representative of that time. This depth of knowledge enriches your collecting experience and adds value to your collection.

Acquiring coins for your themed collection can be one of the most exciting aspects of numismatics. Start by setting goals for your collection. Decide if you want to focus on a specific country, period, or a wide range of items that fit your theme. Create a wish list of coins you aim to acquire and prioritize based on their importance, rarity, or any other criteria you deem significant.

When purchasing coins, always keep your theme in mind. Each coin you add should contribute to the narrative you are building. Be patient and selective, as creating a meaningful collection is a marathon, not a sprint.

Finally, consider how you want to share your collection with others. Displaying your collection is about showcasing your coins and telling their story. Creative displays incorporating descriptions, maps, or historical context can be particularly effective. For example, arranging coins chronologically or according to the geographic region can help viewers appreciate your theme's historical progression or broad impact.

Creating an online gallery or a digital tour of your collection can reach a wider audience and connect you with other collectors who share your interests. This can also provide a platform for interactive learning, where viewers can click on individual coins to learn more about their history and significance.

In thematic collecting, every coin tells a part of a story. By selecting a meaningful theme, researching deeply, carefully acquiring, and creatively displaying your collection, you transform your numismatic activity into a profound expression of your interests and passions.

Collecting Foreign Coins

If your passion for coins has you gazing beyond the borders of your own country, collecting foreign coins can be a thrilling expansion of your collection. This aspect of coin collecting opens up a spectrum of designs, histories, and cultures, making each addition to your collection a doorway to a different part of the world. As you consider diving into the vast ocean of foreign coins, it's like setting sail on an exploratory voyage where each coin is a discovery, and each country's mint holds secrets waiting to be uncovered.

The allure of foreign coins lies in their diversity. From the intricate artistry of the Japanese yen to the historical narratives embossed on European euros, each coin brings a story of its homeland. This exploration can start with countries that have historical or personal significance to you. Perhaps you have roots in another country, or you've traveled somewhere that left a lasting impression. Starting your collection with coins from these places can add a personal connection and meaning. As you grow more comfortable and curious, you might branch out to historically rich regions less known to you. For example, collecting coins from ancient civilizations like those from the Middle East or Latin America can provide a tangible link to the past civilizations of these regions.

As you expand your collection, consider joining international numismatic clubs or online forums where fellow collectors share insights and trade coins. These communities can be invaluable for learning about the nuances of foreign coins. They offer a platform to discuss, exchange, and even purchase or sell coins, providing a broader scope and greater depth to your collection. Engaging with these communities also helps understand the current values and demand for certain coins, guiding your collecting decisions.

When collecting coins from other countries, staying informed about the legal aspects of importing numismatic items is crucial. Different countries have various regulations regarding exporting and importing historical and valuable items, including coins. Some nations might have strict rules against exporting ancient coins, considering them national treasures. Ensuring you comply with all laws is essential to avoid repercussions and ethically support historic preservation.

Before acquiring coins from another country, it's advisable to consult with customs officials or a legal expert who understands international laws regarding numismatic items. Reputable coin dealers and auction houses usually understand these legalities well. They can guide you in acquiring foreign coins legally and ethically. Always ensure that your acquisitions have the necessary documentation that certifies legal procurement and export, safeguarding your collection's integrity.

Discovering reliable sources to purchase foreign coins is a cornerstone of building a diverse and valuable collection. Start with well-established international auction houses with a reputation for authenticity and legality. These platforms often offer coins from around the globe and provide detailed catalogs and provenance (record of ownership) for each item. For more direct sourcing, consider visiting international coin shows and expos.

As for domestic coins, online platforms can also be a rich resource for acquiring foreign coins. Websites like eBay and specialized numismatic sites have sections dedicated to coins from specific countries or regions. When dealing with sellers from other countries, consider the payment methods and shipping arrangements. As mentioned, use secure payment options and insist on insured and trackable shipping methods to protect your purchases.

Understanding the culture and history of the coins you collect adds richness and appreciation to your hobby. Researching the political history, art, and culture of the countries whose coins you collect can provide deeper insights into your collection. Learning about the historical events that influenced the design of British pound coins during the Victorian era or understanding the symbolism behind the animals depicted on South African rand coins can transform your collection from a series of acquisitions into a curated exhibition of global history.

Libraries, museums, and academic institutions can be valuable resources for this kind of research. Many offer access to specialized books, journals, and exhibits on numismatics and history. Online scholarly databases and digital museums also provide access to a wealth of information that can be accessed from all over the world, making it easier to delve into the histories of countries whose coins you are collecting. Each coin you acquire has a story to tell and a history to cherish.

Precious Metal Collecting

Gold and silver coins are more than mere financial investments; they are timeless pieces of art and history. The allure of these metals extends far beyond their shimmering surfaces. They have captivated people's imaginations across various cultures and eras, symbolizing wealth, power, and enduring value. The intrinsic value of these metals means that these coins typically maintain a baseline market value based on their metal content alone, which can provide a sense of security in your collecting endeavors. Beyond this, the designs, mint marks, and historical contexts accompanying these coins add layers of interest and potential value. Each coin you collect is a piece of art and a part of history, enhancing your collection's emotional connection and value.

The first step when collecting gold and silver coins is learning to assess their value accurately. This process goes beyond just admiring their beauty. Start by understanding the purity of the metal. Gold coins, for instance, can range from 22-karat, like the classic American Eagle gold coins, to 24-karat, like the Canadian Gold Maple Leaf. The purity directly affects the coin's intrinsic metal value. However, the weight of the coin also plays a crucial role. Coins are typically weighed in troy ounces, and knowing the exact weight helps calculate the bullion value, which is the baseline value of the coin based on its precious metal content.

The value of gold and silver coins often exceeds their bullion value, especially if they are rare or from a significant historical period. The year of minting, the coin's condition, and its rarity are all factors to consider. Coins minted in limited quantities or with little historical significance can fetch prices above their intrinsic metal value many times. A silver coin from a historic shipwreck or a gold coin from a limited mintage to commemorate an important event carries a premium due to its story and scarcity. Understanding the historical context of these coins adds depth and interest to your collection, making it more than just a financial investment.

Timing your purchases and sales of precious metal coins can significantly impact the financial outcome of your collecting activities. The prices of gold and silver fluctuate daily based on market conditions influenced by factors like political stability, economic performance, and changes in supply and demand. Observing these trends will help you buy when prices are lower and sell when they peak. Subscribing to financial news feeds, following commodities markets, and consulting with financial experts specializing in precious metals can aid in making informed decisions. While the allure of timing the market perfectly is strong, a more sustainable approach is to buy steadily, aligning with your overall collecting goals and budget considerations.

In your journey through the fascinating realm of gold and silver coin collecting, each piece you add brings potential for future appreciation. These coins are not merely passive pieces to be admired but active participants in their times' economic and historical tapestries. Whether you're drawn to the sparkle of gold or the allure of silver, collecting these coins offers a fulfilling path that connects the beauty of numismatics with the tangible values of precious metals. As you continue to explore and grow your collection, consider each addition a safeguard of wealth and a celebration of the history of gold and silver.

Modern vs Vintage:

Every enthusiast faces a pivotal decision in coin collecting: should the focus be on gleaming modern issues or the time-honored vintage pieces? Each category offers its allure and challenges. Modern coins often dazzle with their pristine condition and innovative designs. In contrast, vintage coins whisper tales of the past, bearing marks of history that no new mint can replicate. Understanding the pros and cons, investment potential, and aesthetic considerations will guide you in shaping a collection that resonates with your personal taste and goals.

Modern coins are typically those minted in recent years, often equipped with the latest minting technology, which allows for intricate designs and enhanced security features like holograms or colorized elements. One significant advantage is their availability; you can often purchase these coins directly from mints or authorized dealers at face value or for a small premium. This accessibility makes them a fantastic starting point for new collectors. However, the flip side is that their immediate investment return can be limited because they are so readily available. Most modern coins will only see a significant increase in value over a short period if they are part of a limited edition or a special commemorative series.

Vintage coins carry the mystique of the past, potentially including rare pieces that have survived wars, economic upheavals, and the passage of time. These coins are not just metal; they are historical artifacts. The hunt for such coins can be thrilling, involving visits to antique shops, estate sales, and auctions where you might unearth a coin that hasn't seen the light of day for decades. These coins' rarity and historical value can make them excellent investment vehicles. However, the challenge lies in their acquisition. Vintage coins can be harder to find, require more knowledge to verify authenticity, and often demand a higher initial investment, posing a barrier for those just beginning their collecting journey.

From an investment standpoint, both modern and vintage coins have their merits. Modern limited editions or specially minted series can appreciate quickly if there is high demand. Modern commemorative coins issued for events like the Olympics can become highly sought-after by collectors. The right vintage coins have proven to be reliable long-term investments. Coins from historical periods of significance, especially those in limited quantity or the last of their kind, tend to appreciate as they become scarcer and more collectors enter the market.

When considering coins for investment, consider how easily the coin can be sold when desired. The more common modern coins might only fetch a high price if they are rare editions. Vintage coins have a smaller pool of potential buyers, but those buyers may be willing to pay a premium for rare items. In either case, the condition of the coin significantly impacts its value. Whether modern or vintage, a well-preserved coin can sometimes command an impressive price based on its state.

A coin's aesthetic appeal and historical significance often play an essential role in deciding whether to collect modern or vintage pieces. Modern coins can be stunning, with mints increasingly using new technologies to create stunning visual effects that old mints could only dream of. These coins often reflect contemporary themes and ideals, capturing the spirit of the age in which they are minted.

While vintage coins may not always boast the same artistic detail as modern issues, they carry a natural historical weight. Each wear mark, each fading of the design, tells a story of where the coin has been and the hands it has passed through. For many collectors, this historical narrative is where the true beauty of coin collecting lies.

As this chapter concludes, remember that each coin you choose brings its own story and beauty to your collection, whether modern or vintage. Your chosen path should resonate with your interests and the narrative you wish to create through your collection.

The Collector's Mindset

Each collector chooses a unique blend of motivations. This chapter delves into the psychological landscape of coin collecting, understanding its impacts on our emotions, our sense of legacy, and how we navigate the hobby's ups and downs.

The Psychology Behind Coin Collecting

For many, coin collecting is not just a pastime. There's a unique thrill in the hunt, a serene joy in organizing a growing collection, and a feeling of peace in simply examining the fine details of a coin, appreciating its journey through time. These moments provide a sanctuary from the fast pace of modern life, offering a space where you can slow down, dive deep, and reconnect with yourself. Moreover, the act of collecting can become a meditative practice. As you sort through coins, research their origins, and carefully place them in their designated spots, you are also centering yourself, fostering a sense of calm and order that extends beyond the hobby.

Why do we collect? Psychological theories suggest that collecting fulfills a basic human instinct to gather and store items that ensure survival and comfort. In modern times, though survival isn't directly linked to coin collecting, the underlying drive remains. It taps into our need for control, our desire for knowledge, and our quest for beauty. Collecting can trigger the reward mechanism in our brains. Each new addition to your collection can feel like a small victory, a tangible proof of your dedication and skill, boosting your mood and self-esteem.

Many collectors see their collections not just for enjoyment but as a legacy to pass on. Whether it's to family members, museums, or educational institutions, the idea of your coins being appreciated by future generations can give your hobby a more profound sense of purpose. This forward-looking aspect of collecting encourages collectors to think more critically about what they collect and how they maintain their collections, ensuring their legacy is durable and meaningful. The emotional weight of building a legacy can add a layer to your collecting experience, making each choice more significant and each discovery more rewarding.

As with any passionate endeavor, coin collecting comes with highs and lows. Disappointment may come in many forms: a missed opportunity at an auction, a deal that fell through, or the discovery of a flaw in a coin previously thought to be in mint condition. Handling these moments gracefully is crucial to maintaining your joy in collecting. It is good to acknowledge your feelings of disappointment. This is a natural part of deeply investing in something you care about.

As you build your collection, these psychological insights can guide you to a more fulfilling and meaningful engagement with your numismatic journey, enriching every step with a greater awareness of both the joys and challenges of the collector's path.

The Long Game of Coin Collecting

In coin collecting, patience is a fundamental element that can significantly influence the depth and enjoyment of your hobby. Patience allows your collection to flourish and evolve, sometimes in unexpected and rewarding ways. The nature of coin collecting often involves:

- Waiting for the right coin to appear.

- Waiting for the perfect sale.

- Wait as your knowledge and appreciation of your collection deepen.

If embraced correctly, this waiting creates a more thoughtful approach to collecting.

Patience is not just a virtue in the realm of coin collecting; it's a necessity, especially in the early stages. There's often a natural urge to rapidly expand your collection, to fill it with various pieces that seem appealing. However, the seasoned collector knows true satisfaction comes from understanding each piece's story. This understanding requires patience, as it involves research, discussions with other collectors, and sometimes, just sitting with your collection and observing the details of each coin, noting the slight variations and unique marks that tell of its journey through time.

Setting long-term goals for your collection is not just a task; it's an exercise in envisioning the future you want for your collection. These goals can be as varied as the collectors themselves. Perhaps you aim to complete a series of coins from a specific era or desire to secure rare pieces known only to exist in limited numbers. Whatever your aims, setting these goals gives your collecting a direction and a purpose. It transforms random purchasing into a curated endeavor that slowly but steadily builds toward a well-defined objective.

When faced with setbacks, take a step back and assess the situation calmly. Reflect on what can be learned from the experience. You need to refine your bidding strategies at auction or consult more rigorously with experts before making a purchase. Each disappointment carries a lesson that can refine your approach to collecting, making you more adept and informed. Also, remind yourself of the successes you've had and the pieces you have successfully acquired. This can be a soothing balm on the sting of recent frustrations and can reinvigorate your passion for the hobby.

In the pursuit of long-term goals, it's not just important; it's crucial to recognize and celebrate the small victories along the way. Each new addition to your collection, each successful identification of a rare coin, and each fruitful exchange with fellow collectors are milestones worth acknowledging. These small wins are not just affirmations of your growing expertise and commitment to your hobby; they are the fuel that keeps your passion burning.

Consider creating a ritual around these celebrations. Perhaps you could photograph each new coin and add it to a digital journal chronicling the growth of your collection. Or maybe you could share your successes with a community of fellow collectors, exchanging stories and insights that deepen your shared passion for numismatics. These celebrations enhance your enjoyment of coin collecting and build a narrative of progress and discovery.

You develop a deeply meaningful and valuable collection of coins by cultivating patience through thoughtful goal setting, wisely managing frustrations, and celebrating each achievement. Each coin, decision, and pause in the rush of life contributes to a hobby that is as rich in history as it is in personal satisfaction.

The Joy of Unearthing Hidden Gems

Picture the rush of excitement when, amidst a seemingly ordinary collection, you stumble upon a coin that turns out to be a rare, long-sought-after gem. This moment of discovery is what many coin collectors dream of—finding a piece that not only adds unique value to their collection but also brings an exhilarating story of success. Such moments are not purely based on luck; they're often the result of diligent research, keen observation, and a network of fellow enthusiasts who share your passion for numismatics.

Each coin in your collection holds a story, but some are particularly special. These are the stories of unexpected discoveries. Coins found in forgotten family heirlooms picked up at flea markets for just pennies or identified in a friend's collection as more than just a simple piece of metal. Consider a collector who discovers a rare 1913 Liberty Head nickel in a box of old coins bought at an estate sale. The thrill of realizing that you are holding a piece of history, one of only a handful, is indescribable. These moments are celebratory milestones in a collector's life. They reaffirm the joy of the hunt and the potential for surprise in every corner of this hobby.

The journey to finding hidden gems begins with a groundwork of research and exploration. The more you know, the better equipped you are to spot potential treasures. Immerse yourself in the history of the coins that intrigue you. Learn about the eras they come from, the mints that produced them, and the historical contexts that may affect their rarity and value. This knowledge will be your compass in the vast world of coin collecting.

Connecting with other coin collectors can significantly increase your chances of discovering hidden gems. Fellow enthusiasts not only share their knowledge but may also offer leads on where to find rare coins or sell pieces from their collections that could be the gems you are searching for. Networking can also be about building friendships and a support system within the collecting community. Established connections can sometimes grant you access to private sales and auctions where rare coins are available, places you might have yet to discover on your own.

Once you've made a notable discovery, documenting it thoroughly is not just a task but a crucial step. Maintaining detailed records of where, when, and how you found your coin, along with its historical background and current condition, not only preserves the context of the find but also enhances the coin's value for future transactions or evaluations. Consider creating a digital archive of new discoveries, with photos, descriptions, and scans of any associated documents or certificates of authenticity. This practice will benefit you and contribute to the collective knowledge of the coin-collecting community.

Sharing your discoveries with the collecting community can also be rewarding. It can help you connect with others who share your passion and might lead to new information or opportunities. Sharing your story isn't just about showcasing your success; it's about contributing to the collective knowledge and enthusiasm that fuels the hobby of coin collecting.

Community and Connection

As mentioned earlier, the coin collecting community is open to helping beginners. The first step in tapping into the communal aspects of coin collecting is to identify the right group that aligns with your interests and goals. Start by exploring local clubs in your area. These are often listed in town halls and libraries or searchable online. Local clubs provide the advantage of geographic proximity and offer regular meetings and events where you can physically handle coins, exchange information, and participate in discussions or trades. If your interests are more niche or you prefer the convenience of accessing a community from your home, online forums and social media groups present a valuable alternative. Platforms such as Reddit, Facebook, and specialized numismatic websites host various groups dedicated to every aspect of coin collecting. Here, you can connect with global experts and hobbyists who share your specific interests, whether you're into ancient Roman coins or modern commemorative issues.

When selecting a community, consider the group's activity level, the expertise of its members, and the frequency of their interactions. A vibrant, active community with regular discussions, meet-ups, and shared resources can provide continuous learning and encouragement. Attend a few sessions or participate in online discussions to gauge the community's compatibility with your collecting philosophy and personal demeanor.

Communities foster friendships based on shared interests. These relationships can be profoundly rewarding, providing companionship, a sense of belonging, and mutual support. In a community, your hobby becomes part of a larger narrative, enriched by the stories and experiences of others. These connections often lead to collaborative opportunities such as organizing exhibitions or even starting joint ventures in coin collecting.

As you grow in your coin collecting capabilities, consider giving back to the community. Sharing your understanding and experiences can be fulfilling, and your contributions help sustain the community's vibrancy. You might volunteer to give a talk on a particular topic, write articles for the community newsletter, or offer to mentor newer members. Organizing or participating in community events enriches the community's offerings and establishes you as an active and valued member.

The wisdom of a community is one of its greatest assets. Engaging with fellow collectors allows you to learn from their successes and mistakes, inspiring you to improve your collecting strategy. It's an ongoing process of discovery where every conversation can reveal a new perspective or a piece of advice that could significantly impact your collecting strategy. Listen actively and keep an open mind. Even collectors with very different interests from yours can provide universally applicable insights.

In this chapter, we explored how integrating into the coin collecting community can dramatically enhance your experience of the hobby. From finding the right group to actively participating and learning from collective wisdom, each aspect of community interaction contributes to a richer, more connected approach to collecting. As this is so important, we will explore more aspects of this community later in the book. As we transition to the next chapter, we'll delve deeper into aspects of the digital world of coin collection.

Navigating the Digital World

Imagine stepping into a vast library, where instead of books, each shelf is filled with digital records and catalogs of coins from every corner of the globe. This digital realm offers tools and resources to transform how you explore, understand, and manage your coin collection. As we venture into this online universe, you'll discover how to harness the power of the internet to expand your numismatic knowledge and refine your collector's instincts.

Utilizing Online Catalogs for Research

Online catalogs are like having a seasoned numismatist at your fingertips, ready to provide instant insights into countless coins. These digital resources offer many benefits. They provide detailed information about each coin, including the year of minting, history, and even the detail of variations in design that might not be noticeable to the untrained eye. They often include high-resolution images, allowing you to examine coins as if they were right before you.

For the novice collector, this access is invaluable. It means you can quickly identify coins you come across or are considering purchasing. More so, these catalogs often include valuation data, which is updated regularly, ensuring you have the latest information to help you make informed buying or selling decisions. This aspect is crucial to avoid overpaying for coins or selling your treasures for less than their worth.

Navigating through the many available online catalogs can be daunting. However, specific databases stand out for their reliability and comprehensiveness. For instance, the Numismatic Guaranty Corporation (NGC) offers an extensive online coin database widely respected for its accuracy and user-friendly interface. Another invaluable resource is the Professional Coin Grading Service (PCGS) CoinFacts. This service provides information on American coins, including historical data and current market values.

For those interested in world coins, the World Coin Gallery offers an expansive online catalog covering many countries and coinage systems. Similarly, the European Coin Database is an excellent resource for collectors focusing on European mints, offering detailed images and descriptions of coins from various European nations.

Using these online catalogs effectively can empower you to appraise your coins or potential acquisitions accurately. Search for your coin using specific criteria such as the year, country, and denomination. Once you find your coin, review the provided information carefully. Compare your coin's condition to the grading images and descriptions in the catalog. This comparison will give you an idea of where your coin stands and how that grade affects its value.

Many of these catalogs offer historical price data, showing how the value of a particular coin has changed over time. This information can be crucial when deciding whether to buy, hold, or sell a coin, as it provides insight into potential future value trends.

It is wise to cross-reference details from multiple online catalogs to ensure the accuracy and completeness of the information you gather. This practice helps verify the consistency of the data and protects against relying on potentially incorrect or outdated information. For instance, if you find an error in the reported mint year of a coin between two databases, further research or consultation with an expert may be necessary to resolve the conflict.

Cross-referencing gives a more holistic view of your coin's standing in the global market. Different catalogs might highlight various aspects of a coin, such as its historical significance or rarity, providing a richer understanding of what makes your coin special and how those factors influence its value.

To practice your skills in using and cross-referencing online catalogs:

1. Select a coin from your collection and look it up in at least two databases.

2. Compare the information provided on each site, focusing on aspects such as mint date, mint mark, historical context, and current valuation.

3. Note any discrepancies and conduct further research to clarify these differences.

This exercise will improve your research skills and deepen your appreciation of the complexities and nuances of coin collecting.

In this digital age, your ability to navigate online resources effectively can significantly enhance your efficiency and success as a coin collector. As you continue to explore the vastness of online catalogs and databases, remember that each click and each search is a step toward becoming a more knowledgeable and confident numismatist.

Digital Tools for Coin Collecting

As you delve deeper into the fascinating hobby of coin collecting, you'll find that embracing digital tools can significantly streamline and enhance your experience. These tools are designed with both the beginner and seasoned collector in mind, providing solutions that simplify the management of your collection and enrich your interaction with each piece you own. Let's explore some of the most effective digital aids available today and how they can transform your approach to collecting.

Apps and software tailored for coin collectors can be a real game-changer. These digital tools offer a plethora of functionalities, from cataloging your coins and tracking their value to connecting you with a vibrant community of collectors and experts worldwide. Apps like Coinoscope, Coinsnap, and Coin ID use image recognition technology to identify coins just by taking a photo. This can be incredibly useful when deciphering the details of a newly acquired piece or verifying coins at auctions or shops. Other software, like Numista, allows you to manage your collection online, providing tools to organize, track, and even trade coins with a global community. These platforms often include databases with detailed information about a wide array of coins, fostering a sense of connection and learning within the community.

Photographing your coins is another crucial skill that digital tools can help with. Good photography captures the beauty and detail of your coins and can aid in documentation, online sharing, or sale. To get the best results, use a high-resolution camera (many new cell phones have great cameras) and set up proper lighting. Soft, indirect light works best to avoid dark shadows and emphasize the fine details of the coins. A simple setup with a lightbox and a couple of LED lamps can significantly improve the quality of your photos.

Additionally, consider using a macro lens or a macro filter. These allow you to capture close-up details essential for documenting each coin's condition and unique features. When setting up your shot, use a neutral background that doesn't distract from the coin itself, and ensure the coin is entirely in focus to capture as much detail as possible.

Maintaining a digital record of your collection offers numerous benefits. It not only helps in organizing and accessing your coins quickly but also in securing essential data about each piece. Various software options cater to different aspects of collecting. Applications like Exact Change provide comprehensive tools for cataloging your collection, including images, historical data, and current market values. These programs often feature user-friendly interfaces that simplify updating and maintaining your records. A well-organized digital catalog allows you to access information about your collection quickly, prepare for appraisals, or plan your displays for exhibitions. Moreover, having a digital record can be essential for insurance purposes or future sales, providing a detailed account of your collection's worth.

Security should always be a top priority when using digital tools. Always backup your data to safeguard against hardware failures, data corruption, or cyber threats. Use reliable services and software that offer secure data storage options. Cloud storage can be a great choice, as it provides remote access to your data and ensures that a backup is maintained off-site, protecting against physical damage to your devices. Additionally, exercise caution when sharing sensitive information online. When using forums or selling platforms, ensure that if any personal data is transmitted, you're knowledgeable about the privacy policies of the platforms you use. You can feel confident and reassured in your digital coin-collecting practices by prioritizing security.

Integrating these digital tools into your coin-collecting hobby creates a new dimension of efficiency and enjoyment. These technologies simplify the logistical aspects of managing and expanding your collection. Whether through better organization, improved documentation, or more secure data management, digital tools are indispensable for the modern collector.

Engaging with Online Collector Communities

Embarking on the digital journey as a coin collector leads you to the dynamic realm of online communities, where coin enthusiasts from all corners of the world converge. Imagine stepping into a virtual room teeming with fellow numismatists, all sharing your love for coins, each with their unique insights to offer. These platforms, ranging from specialized forums to comprehensive websites, are dedicated to the art and science of coin collecting. By immersing yourself in these communities, you can significantly enhance your collecting experience, gaining access to a treasure trove of knowledge and opportunities.

Consider what you hope to gain from joining such a community. Are you looking for educational resources, opportunities to buy or sell, or the camaraderie of shared interests? Once you have a clear idea, explore popular numismatic websites and forums. Sites like CoinTalk and the Collectors Universe forums are bustling with activity and discussion on various coin-collecting topics. For a more visual and interactive experience, social media such as Facebook and Instagram host numerous coin-collecting groups and pages where members frequently post images of their coins, share stories, and offer advice.

When selecting a community, take the time to observe the interactions and the type of content shared. A good community should not only be active but also welcoming and informative. Join a few and participate passively at first by reading posts and observing discussions. This will help you understand the community's vibe and whether it aligns with your interests and values in coin collecting.

As you delve into these communities, remember that practicing good online etiquette is paramount. The digital world is just as real as the physical one and respectful, thoughtful interactions are the key to fostering positive relationships. Always respond with politeness and consideration, acknowledging that others may hold different opinions. Be clear and concise when posting, whether seeking advice or sharing information. Provide as much relevant information as possible to facilitate meaningful discussions. For example, if you're seeking advice about a specific coin, include clear images and any background information you have. This will enable others to provide more accurate and valuable responses.

Keep an open mind when engaging in debates or discussions. The diversity within these communities can be one of the most powerful learning tools. Seize these opportunities to broaden your understanding and deepen your knowledge of numismatics.

Online communities are goldmines of information, and you can learn immensely by participating actively. Many experienced collectors and professionals frequent these forums and are often generous with their knowledge. Take advantage of this by asking well-thought-out questions and tapping into the collective wisdom available. Many communities also organize virtual events such as webinars, live talks with experts, and online workshops that can provide deeper insights into specific aspects of coin collecting.

Moreover, these platforms can be excellent resources for staying informed on market trends and news in the numismatic world. Members often share updates about new coin releases, auction results, and market fluctuations, which can help you make informed decisions about your collection.

Engaging with online collector communities opens up possibilities, from expanding your knowledge and network to enhancing your collection and participation in the wider numismatic world. As you navigate these digital platforms, each interaction is a step towards building a richer, more connected experience in coin collecting.

Creating a Digital Inventory of Your Collection

Having a meticulously organized record of your coin collection that you can access instantly is the convenience a digital inventory offers. This type of system simplifies your collection management and enhances your ability to share and showcase your coins with others. One significant advantage is the ease of access; whether you're meeting with fellow collectors, discussing a potential sale, or want to admire your collection during a lunch break, your entire catalog is just a few clicks away. A well-organized digital inventory helps keep track of various aspects of your collection, such as purchase dates, prices, and conditions, making it easier to see trends and make informed decisions about future acquisitions or sales.

A digital inventory reduces the risk of human error and loss from physical record-keeping. It is a secure backup in cases of physical damage to your collection or unforeseen events like theft. This system also allows for dynamic updating and editing, particularly useful as your collection grows and changes over time. You can quickly add new acquisitions, modify existing entries, or remove items sold or traded, ensuring that your inventory is always current and reflects your actual collection.

Setting up a digital inventory might seem daunting initially. Still, with the right tools and a bit of organization, it can be a straightforward and rewarding process. Begin by choosing the right software or app that suits your needs. Several options are available, ranging from specialized coin-collecting software like Trove Software's CoinManage, which offers detailed templates and fields tailored to numismatics, to more general database software like Microsoft Access, which can be customized extensively.

When setting up your inventory, include vital data that will help you track and manage your collection efficiently. Essential details typically include the coin's country of origin, year of minting, denomination, condition, and any unique features or historical significance. Recording the purchase price, estimated value, and any sales or trades involving the coin is also helpful. Including high-quality images of each coin can enhance your inventory, making it easier to review or share your collection visually.

Start by entering coins you are most familiar with, gradually adding more items as you get comfortable with the system. Make sure to categorize your coins by era, region, or theme in a way that makes sense for your collecting style. This keeps your inventory organized and makes it easier to locate specific items when needed.

Frequent updates are critical to make sure your digital inventory remains a valuable tool. Set a routine to review and update your inventory. During each update session, add new coins, adjust the details of existing entries as needed, and remove any coins no longer in your collection. Also, revisit the estimated values of your coins periodically. Market values can change based on different factors, and keeping your inventory current with these changes can be vital, especially if you use the information for insurance or investment purposes.

It's also wise to perform regular backups of your digital inventory. Use cloud storage services to ensure that you have an off-site backup in case of computer failure or data loss. This redundancy can protect your collection data and give you peace of mind knowing your detailed records are safe.

A comprehensive and up-to-date digital inventory can significantly streamline the process of appraising your collection or preparing for sales. When you need an appraisal for insurance purposes or are considering selling part of your collection, having detailed records readily available can expedite the process and ensure accurate evaluations. Appraisers and potential buyers often request detailed information on each piece. With a digital inventory, this information can be shared quickly and professionally, increasing the credibility of your data and potentially enhancing the value of your collection.

As you continue to use digital tools in your numismatic activities, remember that a digital inventory is a tool that grows and changes with your collection, enhancing every aspect of your coin-collecting experience. As we turn the page to the next chapter, we'll explore coins as an investment.

Investing in Coins

Like art, coins can be more than just a hobby; they can be a wise and rewarding investment. As you delve deeper into coin collecting, understanding how to approach this aspect can transform your casual interest into a significant financial asset. This chapter will guide you through seeing coins as collectibles and potential keystones in your investment portfolio.

Coins as an Investment

Coins have a unique position in the investment world. They offer the intrinsic value of the materials they are made and historical and numismatic value. This dual nature makes coins particularly appealing as an investment. Over the years, certain coins have shown remarkable appreciation in value, driven by factors such as rarity, demand, and their condition. Consider a coin issued in limited quantities during a historically significant event; such a coin might increase in value not only because of its rarity but also because of its historical importance, which attracts collectors and investors alike.

Coins are often seen as a hedge against inflation. Precious metals like gold and silver, which many coins are made of, have historically maintained their value over time, even as fiat currencies can lose value under economic turbulence. This characteristic makes investing in coins particularly appealing during financial uncertainty, providing security to investors looking to preserve their wealth.

Like all investments, coin investing comes with its own set of risks and rewards. Market volatility can significantly affect the value of coins. Prices can fluctuate based on updates in the precious metals market, shifts in collector demand, and broader economic conditions. The liquidity of coin investments can vary. While some coins can be sold relatively quickly due to high demand, others might take longer to find a buyer, particularly if they appeal to a niche market.

The rewards can be excellent for those who do their research and invest wisely. The key is to understand not only the market but also the coins themselves. Knowledge about the history, rarity, and potential demand for particular coins can lead to informed decisions that pay off. Seasoned collectors know that part of the joy of coin collecting as an investment is this very challenge: the thrill of the hunt for coins that hold promise, not just as beautiful objects to behold but as assets that might appreciate in value.

Including coins in your investment portfolio can also aid in diversification, which is crucial for managing investment risk. Just as you diversify your portfolio with a combination of stocks, bonds, and real estate, adding coins can provide an alternative asset class that behaves differently from traditional financial instruments. This diversification can smooth out returns and buffer against volatility in other parts of your portfolio.

Consider different types of coins for effective diversification. You might mix bullion coins, which are valued primarily for their precious metal content, with rare numismatic coins, which can appreciate based on factors like rarity, historical significance, and condition. This strategy can help balance the liquidity of your investments in coins, as bullion coins are generally easier to sell than rare numismatic coins.

Not all coins are created equal in the eyes of an investor. Investment-grade coins hold the potential to increase in value over time. These coins typically share several attributes: they are rare, in excellent condition (often with a high grade from a reputable grading service), and have a demand among collectors and investors. Identifying such coins requires a keen eye and a deep understanding of what makes a coin desirable.

For beginners, starting with coins that are more commonly recognized as valuable investments is advisable. Gold and silver bullion coins issued by reputable mints like the U.S. Mint, Royal Canadian Mint, or The Royal Mint in the U.K. are usually a safe bet. These coins are backed by their respective governments, guaranteeing their purity and weight. As you gain more experience and knowledge, you might explore more niche areas, such as ancient coins or specific historical series, each of which requires more specialized expertise but can also offer unique opportunities for appreciation.

Embracing coin collecting as a hobby and an investment opens up new avenues for personal and financial growth. Each coin you add to your collection can serve as a stepping stone towards achieving broader financial goals, making the hobby both rewarding and profitable.

When to Buy and Sell

Navigating the numismatic market requires more than just an understanding of coins; it demands a keen sense of timing. Knowing when to buy and sell will significantly impact the returns on your investments. Imagine you're a surfer trying to catch the perfect wave: timing your move too early or too late could mean missing out on the ride of a lifetime. Similarly, in coin collecting, aligning your buying and selling decisions with market cycles and trends can lead to lucrative outcomes or help you avoid losses during downturns.

Effective market timing starts with a strategy that combines research, observation, and patience. One practical approach is to monitor upcoming auctions and major numismatic events. These events often set trends in the market, influencing prices and demand for certain types of coins. If a particularly rare coin fetches a record price at auction, it could raise interest and values for similar coins. By focusing on these events, you can plan your buying or selling strategies around them, capitalizing on the heightened market activity.

Another strategy involves seasonal buying and selling. Just like retail markets, the numismatic market can experience seasonal fluctuations. Often, the market sees increased activity around the end of the year, coinciding with holidays when people might buy coins as gifts. Understanding these patterns can help you decide the best times to sell when buyer interest is peaking. Conversely, buying during slower periods, when tax bills are due, and collectors are selling parts of their collections to fund payments, might allow you to purchase coins at lower prices.

The numismatic market is not immune to cycles of boom and bust, influenced by broader economic conditions, collector interest, and other external factors. These cycles can affect the value of coins, with periods of high demand driving prices up and times of low interest or economic downturn causing them to dip. By recognizing where the market is in its cycle, you can make better and more informed decisions about when to buy or sell.

During a market upswing, rare coins might see significant appreciation in value. This could be an excellent time to evaluate your collection and consider selling coins that have reached peak values. Conversely, during downturns, you might find opportunities to buy undervalued coins that have the potential to increase in value as the market recovers. Keeping an eye on economic indicators, collector interest trends, and historical price movements of coins can provide clues about the current market cycle phase.

To spot these cycles and trends, you need to be aware of the indicators that signal shifts in the market. Price indices for coins, similar to stock market indices, can show how coin prices are moving overall. Publications and websites that track coin sales and auction results can also offer valuable data. A sudden price spike for a particular coin type could indicate growing interest and a potential investment opportunity.

Keep an eye on the broader economy. Factors such as inflation, interest, and currency fluctuations can influence collectible markets. If inflation is high, tangible assets like coins might become more attractive to investors, driving up prices and demand. Being attuned to these broader economic conditions can give you a strategic edge in timing your transactions.

Deciding between long-term and short-term investing strategies in coin collecting depends mainly on your personal goals and risk tolerance. Long-term investing typically involves holding onto coins for years or even decades. This approach will be beneficial as it allows the value of the coins to appreciate over time, potentially yielding higher returns when you decide to sell. It also minimizes the impact of short-term market volatility on your investment.

Short-term investing might involve buying and selling coins more frequently, capitalizing on short-term trends or fluctuations in the market. This strategy can be more labor-intensive and riskier, requiring you to closely monitor market conditions and make timely decisions. However, it can also offer quicker returns and greater flexibility in managing your investment portfolio.

Both strategies have their merits, and many collectors choose a combination of the two, holding some coins for long-term appreciation while trading others for short-term gains. Your choice might depend on how actively you want to manage your investments, your financial goals, and what risk you are comfortable taking.

Mastering the art of timing in the coin market enhances your profit potential. Each purchase and sale becomes a calculated move in your ongoing adventure in coin collecting, enriching your experience with rewards.

Estate Planning with Your Coin Collection

When you consider your coin collection, you might see it as a hobby and a part of your legacy. It is a treasure of history and personal achievement you can pass on. Integrating your collection into your estate plan is a thoughtful process, blending the practical with the sentimental. It ensures that your coins are appreciated and cared for even when you can no longer manage them yourself. Let's explore how you can ensure your collection continues to be a source of joy and value.

Incorporating your coin collection into your estate plan requires careful consideration and planning. The first step is to ensure that your collection is well-documented, as mentioned. This documentation should include detailed descriptions of each coin, including its condition, purchase price, current estimated value, and any historical significance. It's also wise to include high-quality photographs and any appraisals or certificates of authenticity you have. This comprehensive record will be invaluable to your heirs and the executors of your estate, helping them understand the value of your collection and how best to manage or disperse it.

Valuation is a critical component of this documentation. The value of coins can change based on current market conditions, so it's vital to have up-to-date appraisals. These appraisals should be kept with your estate documents and updated in your estate plan.

Once your collection is documented and valued, you must decide how it will be handled after passing. You can specify precisely how you want your coins distributed in your will or trust. You can leave the entire collection to a single heir, divide it among several beneficiaries, or donate it to a museum or educational institution. Suppose you choose to bequeath it to family members or friends. In that case, it's also helpful to include instructions or wishes on how you hope they will care for or display the collection.

Legal considerations play a significant role when bequeathing a coin collection. Depending on where you live, specific laws may exist regarding the inheritance and taxation of collectibles. In some jurisdictions, the value of a coin collection may be subject to estate taxes, which could impact how much your heirs receive. It's critical to consult with an attorney specializing in estate planning to navigate these laws effectively. They can help you structure your estate to minimize tax burdens and align with your wishes.

Suppose you plan to leave your collection to someone who lives in another country. In that case, international laws regarding the transfer of assets should be considered. Legal and tax implications can vary significantly from one country to another, and you'll need expert advice to avoid potential complications.

Selecting heirs for your coin collection is a deeply personal decision beyond mere legalities. It's about finding someone who will value the coins as much as you do. When choosing an heir for your collection, consider their interest in numismatics, financial acumen, and ability to care for it. Discussing your plans with potential heirs beforehand may help gauge their interest and willingness to take on the responsibility. This conversation can also be an opportunity to share your knowledge and passion for the collection, potentially deepening their appreciation.

If you suspect that your chosen heirs might not be interested in maintaining the collection, consider setting up a trust to manage the collection on their behalf. A trust can provide professional management and care for the collection, with eventual distribution or sale provisions. This can be a way to preserve the collection's value and ensure it is handled appropriately, even if the ultimate beneficiaries are not collectors themselves.

Sometimes, you might decide that the best option is for your collection to be sold after your passing. If this is your choice, providing clear instructions on handling the sale is essential. You might specify particular dealers or auction houses to be used or set minimum prices for certain items to ensure they are sold for at least their market value. Suppose you are concerned about your heirs' ability to manage such a sale. In that case, you might appoint a trusted advisor or executor with experience in numismatics to oversee the process.

Auctions are often the best way to achieve fair market value for rare or valuable coins. Many major auction houses have experts in numismatics who can help assess the collection and attract the right buyers. Consider selling the collection to a reputable dealer if you prefer a quicker or more private sale. Dealers can offer immediate payment, but the prices may be lower than what might be achieved at auction.

As you weave your coin collection into your estate planning, you organize assets and ensure the continuation of a legacy. Whether preserved by heirs, displayed in a museum, or thoughtfully sold to other passionate collectors, your coins can continue to tell their stories long into the future, a testament to your care and dedication.

Taxes and Your Coin Collection

Understanding the tax implications becomes crucial when viewing your coin collection not just as a hobby but as a financial investment. Like any asset that can appreciate in value, coins can attract attention from tax authorities, mainly when you buy or sell them. Let's ease into this topic, which might seem daunting at first, by breaking down the essentials of taxation in the context of coin collecting.

Capital gains tax is the most direct tax implication you might encounter with your coin collection. This tax is levied on the profit from selling your coins at a larger price than you purchased them. If you bought a coin for $500 and later sold it for $1,500, you'd be liable for tax on the $1,000 profit. The rate at which you are taxed can depend on how long you hold the coin. In many regions, assets held for more extended periods, typically over a year, are subject to long-term capital gains tax, which has a smaller tax rate than short-term gains from assets held for shorter periods.

It's also important to consider how these taxes vary depending on location. Different states or countries have different rules regarding the taxation of collectibles. Some might even offer exemptions or reduced rates under certain conditions, such as if the sale is part of settling an estate or if the proceeds are donated to charity.

One of the most effective ways to manage potential tax liabilities is by keeping meticulous records of your coin transactions. This includes documenting the purchase date, purchase price, sale price, and any expenses or costs related to the acquisition or sale of the coins, such as auction fees or restoration costs. These records help calculate capital gains accurately and serve as essential proof if authorities question your tax filings. As mentioned a few times, maintaining receipts, appraisals, and any correspondence related to your coin transactions is advisable in addition to transaction records.

Tax laws can be complex and are often subject to changes that could affect how your coin investments are treated. It is crucial to stay educated about the current tax laws and any potential changes. This might involve regularly checking updates from your tax authority or following news related to finance and investments.

Specific provisions could apply to numismatic collectors. There might be different rules for coins considered numismatic versus those seen primarily as bullion. Understanding these details will help you optimize your tax strategy, potentially saving money and avoiding legal pitfalls.

Given the complexities of tax laws and the significant amounts of money that might be involved, consulting with a tax professional with experience with collectibles and investments is highly recommended. A tax advisor can offer personalized advice tailored to your specific situation. They can help you understand your tax obligations, plan your buying and selling activities to minimize taxes and ensure you comply with all relevant laws.

A tax professional can also be invaluable in more complex scenarios, such as if you're considering passing on your collection to heirs or donating it to a museum. They can guide you through the implications of these decisions, helping you execute your plans in the most tax-efficient manner possible.

Navigating the tax aspects of coin collecting might initially seem like a daunting addition to your hobby. However, with careful planning, diligent record-keeping, and the right professional advice, you can manage these obligations effectively, ensuring that your focus remains on your collection's enjoyment and potential profits. This foundational understanding protects you against possible legal issues. It empowers you to make smarter decisions that enhance the financial benefits of your endeavors.

As we close this chapter on the financial intricacies of coin collecting, remember that each piece in your collection carries potential value that extends beyond the joy of collecting. With the right strategies, This value can significantly contribute to your financial security and legacy. Looking ahead, our journey will take us to add more knowledge and keep you up to date on the future of your hobby.

Expanding Your Numismatic Knowledge

Building your numismatic library, a treasure trove of knowledge that can transform your approach to coin collecting. This chapter delves into the literary world of numismatics, exploring essential resources that can deepen your appreciation and expertise in coin collecting.

Building Your Reference Library

Building a comprehensive numismatic library is like assembling a toolkit; each book serves a specific purpose, helping you to identify, evaluate, and appreciate your coins. After this book, start with cornerstone texts like "A Guide Book of United States Coins" by R.S. Yeoman, commonly known as the "Red Book." This guide offers detailed information on coin prices, grading, and history, making it indispensable for beginners and seasoned collectors. Additionally, the "Standard Catalog of World Coins" by Chester Krause and Clifford Mishler covers coins from 1601 to the present. It provides a global perspective essential for a well-rounded collector.

For those interested in the intricacies of grading, "The Official American Numismatic Association Grading Standards for United States Coins" by Kenneth Bressett and Q. David Bowers offers a detailed visual and descriptive guide to coin grades. This resource can significantly enhance your ability to assess the condition of your coins, a skill fundamental to successful collecting.

Historical texts should be noticed; they offer context that can dramatically enrich your collection. Books such as "Coinage and History of the Roman Empire" by David Vagi bridge the gap between numismatics and historical scholarship, allowing you to see your Roman coins as collectibles and artifacts of a sprawling empire.

The world of numismatics is ever-evolving, with discoveries and market shifts regularly impacting collectors. Subscribing to periodicals such as "Coin World" and "Numismatic News" informs you of the latest trends, auction results, and scholarly articles. These publications can be a window to the numismatic community, offering insights into what other collectors are excited about and how the market is shifting.

Online forums and digital newsletters will also help you keep your finger on the pulse of the numismatic world. Websites like the Professional Numismatists Guild offer updates on market trends and essential numismatic events, which can influence your collecting strategies and investment decisions.

In today's digital age, a wealth of knowledge is available at your fingertips. Online databases and eBooks offer convenient, up-to-date information that can complement your physical library. Websites like the Newman Numismatic Portal provide free access to numerous numismatic literatures, auction catalogs, and magazines, which can be invaluable for research and verification. EBooks such as "U.S. Coin Digest" offer a portable, searchable option for quick reference during auctions or when evaluating potential acquisitions. These digital resources are helpful for specific queries, allowing you to quickly find information without sifting through multiple physical books.

Exploring historical numismatic literature provides insights into the coins themselves and the evolution of the field of numismatics. Older texts, such as "The History of Coin Collecting" by Q. David Bowers, offer a retrospective look at how coin collecting has developed over centuries, including the collectors who have shaped the hobby and the historical contexts that have influenced coin designs and values.

Diving into these historical texts can be incredibly rewarding. They offer a deeper understanding of how numismatics intersects with broader historical trends and events. They can also inspire a greater appreciation for your collection, connecting you with past collectors whose passion for coins has preserved this fascinating hobby through the ages.

As you continue to build your numismatic library, remember that each book and article adds a layer of understanding to your collecting experience. Whether you're flipping through the pages of a dusty old catalog or scrolling through an eBook, you're participating in a centuries-old tradition of learning and discovery that enhances your journey as a collector.

Attending Coin Shows and Auctions

The vibrant scene at a coin show, an event that brings together enthusiasts, experts, and newcomers alike. Attending coin shows can be one of the most enriching experiences for anyone passionate about numismatics. You get to see and handle a wide variety of coins and have the opportunity to meet and interact with other collectors and professionals. These interactions can significantly broaden your understanding of the hobby and lead to lasting friendships and mentorships.

Networking is a crucial element of attending coin shows. These events provide a rare opportunity to meet with dealers, experienced collectors, and numismatic experts face-to-face. Engaging in conversations at these shows can open up new avenues of knowledge and resources. You might learn about lesser-known coins, learn advanced collecting techniques, or discover new tools and accessories to enhance your collecting experience. Building relationships at these events can also lead to future opportunities to buy or sell coins through private deals, often at better rates than found online or in stores due to the mutual trust established.

Coin shows often feature unique buying and selling opportunities. Many shows have "bid boards" or silent auctions, where you can place bids on coins throughout the event, potentially snagging a valuable piece at a competitive price. Additionally, some dealers may bring inventory to a show they don't offer elsewhere, providing access to unique or rare coins. This setting allows you to physically inspect coins before purchasing, an advantage over online buying, where you rely on pictures and descriptions.

Coin auctions in person are thrilling, just like online auctions. Participating in an auction requires a blend of knowledge, strategy, and sometimes a bit of nerve. Before diving into auction bidding, it's essential to do your homework. This means studying the auction catalog thoroughly, identifying items of interest, and understanding their market value and historical significance. It's also wise to set a budget before the auction to avoid getting caught up in the moment and spending more than intended.

Live auctions offer a dynamic experience where you can gauge the interest of other bidders and adjust your strategy accordingly. If you're new to auctions, attending a few without bidding might be beneficial to observe the process and develop an understanding of the pacing and atmosphere.

Due diligence is crucial in both live and online auctions. This includes verifying the authenticity and condition of the coins, understanding the buyer's premiums (additional charges imposed by the auction house), and knowing the return policies. Being well-prepared can significantly enhance your auction experience and chances of success.

Coin shows and auctions are not just about buying and selling but also educational. Many events host seminars and workshops led by numismatic experts, covering topics from coin grading to the latest coin preservation technology. These sessions can provide insights that books or online articles cannot, often allowing for interactive participation and personalized advice.

Panel discussions and lectures at these events can offer deeper dives into specific areas of numismatics, such as the history of a particular type of coin, upcoming market trends, or advanced collecting techniques. These learning opportunities are invaluable for expanding one's knowledge.

Understanding etiquette at coin shows and auctions can significantly enhance your experience. Simple courtesies like asking before handling someone's coins, respecting others' time, and maintaining professionalism during negotiations go a long way in establishing good relationships within the community. Remember, the numismatic community is tight-knit, and your reputation can significantly impact your interactions and opportunities.

Regarding networking, always be ready to introduce yourself and share your interests. Carrying a business card that includes your contact information and collecting interests can facilitate follow-ups and future interactions. Listen as much as you talk; you can learn much from the experiences and stories of other collectors. Consider joining discussions and group activities; these can be fun, enriching, and a fantastic way to meet like-minded people who share your love of coins.

Attending coin shows and participating in auctions bring the historical and communal aspects of coin collecting to life. They offer a dynamic complement to the more solitary aspects of the hobby. As you step into your next coin show or log into an online auction, embrace the community, learn from the collective knowledge present, and enjoy the unique thrill of engaging directly with the vibrant world of numismatics.

Joining Local Numismatic Societies and Clubs

Imagine entering a room filled with fellow coin enthusiasts, each member buzzing with stories about their latest finds, sharing insights into rare coin histories, or offering tips on preserving valuable pieces. This is the vibrant atmosphere you can expect when you join a local numismatic society or club. These organizations are about bringing collectors together. They serve as platforms for education, resource sharing, and fostering community among those passionate about numismatics.

When you start looking for a numismatic society or club to join, consider what aspects of coin collecting excite you the most. Identifying your interests will help you find a group that aligns with your passions. Start by exploring local clubs in your area, which can be found through online directories or coin-collecting forums. Local clubs often offer regular meetings and events, making it easy to get involved and stay active within the community.

International societies might be the perfect fit for those whose interests are more geographically broad or specialized. Organizations like the American Numismatic Association (ANA) offer extensive resources, including online forums, digital libraries, and a calendar of national and international events. Joining such societies can provide you with a wealth of knowledge and connect you to experts and enthusiasts worldwide.

Enrich your collecting experience significantly by joining a numismatic society and accessing resources you might otherwise be missing, such as libraries with dedicated numismatics materials. As a member, enjoy free or discounted access to these resources and exclusive publications that keep you updated on the latest news and research in the field.

Numismatic clubs offer a wealth of educational programs. From beginner courses that cover grading and coin history basics to advanced seminars that explore numismatic science and market trends, there's something for everyone. Workshops led by experienced collectors and professionals provide hands-on learning opportunities that can't be replicated online or in books.

Being part of a numismatic society is more than just a hobby-it's a community. Share your passion with like-minded individuals, trade coins, experiences, knowledge, and friendship. Your relationships within these communities can offer support and encouragement, making your numismatic journey even more rewarding.

International societies often host global conferences and symposiums, providing an opportunity to meet fellow collectors and experts face-to-face. Such events can be a fantastic way to gain deeper insights into the global numismatic landscape and understand the subtleties influencing coin collecting across different cultures and markets. These gatherings often feature auctions and sales of rare and exotic coins, allowing you to acquire pieces not commonly available in your local market.

Joining a numismatic society, whether local or international, opens up chances for learning, sharing, and connecting with others who share your passion for coins. As you dive into this engaging community, you'll find that every meeting, every conversation, and every event adds a valuable layer to your experience as a collector.

The Future of Coin Collecting and Trends to Watch

As we look to the future of coin collecting, it's clear that the landscape is evolving with remarkable speed, influenced by technological advances and a growing awareness of ethical and sustainability practices. Understanding these shifts is essential for anyone involved in numismatics, whether you're a seasoned collector or just beginning to explore this fascinating hobby.

One of the most exciting developments in recent years is the rise of digital numismatics. This isn't just about online auctions or forums—it's about how technology is used to create and track collections digitally. For instance, virtual reality (VR) technology is beginning to enter the numismatic world. It allows collectors to view detailed 3D models of coins from their homes. This technology enhances the collector's experience and serves educational purposes, allowing enthusiasts to interactively learn about the intricacies of coin designs and historical contexts.

Furthermore, alternative collecting, such as cryptocurrency tokens representing physical coins, is gaining traction. These digital tokens, backed by blockchain technology, ensure the authenticity and ownership of a coin without the need for physical possession. This trend particularly appeals to younger collectors comfortable with digital investments and looking for innovative ways to engage with numismatics.

The integration of technology into coin collecting extends beyond digital displays and blockchain. Advanced imaging and scanning technologies are now used to assess and authenticate coins, replacing more subjective, manual inspections with precise, unbiased data. This shift improves the accuracy of coin grading. It increases trust in the buying and selling process, which can often be uncertain regarding a coin's condition and authenticity.

Blockchain technology, in particular, is a game-changer for numismatics. By creating a permanent, unchangeable record of a coin's history, ownership, and authenticity, blockchain provides security and transparency that was previously unattainable. This technology can remove the risk of counterfeit coins circulating in the market, making it safer and more appealing for new collectors to invest in numismatics.

As society becomes conscious of environmental issues and ethical practices, these values are increasingly reflected in coin collecting. Collectors and dealers alike are beginning to prioritize sustainability in the care and preservation of coins, opting for eco-friendly materials in coin storage and reducing the reliance on chemicals in cleaning and restoration processes.

Ethical collecting also involves considering a coin's provenance. Ensuring that coins are legally and ethically acquired has become a priority, particularly in historical coins that may have been looted or illicitly traded. Collectors are now more diligent about verifying the origins of their coins, seeking pieces with clear histories that do not contribute to the destruction of cultural heritage.

Adapting to these trends involves staying informed and open to change. For collectors, this might mean embracing new technologies that enhance the collecting experience or reconsidering the types of coins they collect based on ethical considerations. It also involves being proactive in community discussions about the direction of numismatics, contributing ideas and feedback that can help shape a more sustainable, inclusive future for this hobby.

For those just starting, the evolving landscape of coin collecting offers a dynamic and exciting environment to explore numismatics. It's a time of innovation and transformation, providing new opportunities to engage with history, technology, and global cultures through coin collecting.

As we continue to explore the world of numismatics, it's clear that the future holds exciting possibilities for enhancing personal collections and growing the global collecting community. This evolution promises to unite more people by a shared passion for coins and their stories, ensuring the enduring appeal and relevance of coin collecting for generations to come.

Conclusion

As we draw the curtains on this journey through the captivating realm of coin collecting, I hope you've found this guide informative and inspiring. From starting your collection and understanding the nuances of coin grading to the more advanced realms of collecting and investment strategies, we've traversed a landscape rich with history and opportunity.

Throughout these pages, we've delved into the critical importance of coin grading, experienced the thrill of hunting for those rare, elusive pieces, and learned how to plan and budget our collecting endeavors strategically. We've also explored the vibrant community that makes coin collecting so unique. Now, a community that you're well prepared to join.

Coin collecting isn't just a hobby; it's a continuous journey of learning and discovery. You should keep exploring, attend coin shows, engage in online forums, and connect with other enthusiasts.

Every coin has a story, a chance to expand your appreciation and understanding of this fascinating field.

Now, I urge you to start or expand your collection, connect with fellow collectors, and consider how these precious tokens can fit into your financial planning. Remember, coin collecting is accessible to everyone. It doesn't matter if your budget is modest or you're beginning to learn the ropes. The numismatic world is welcoming to all.

Joining the coin-collecting community offers more than just knowledge. It provides an environment to share your passion and learn from the experiences of others. While challenges include avoiding scams and making informed purchases, the rewards are profound, from the joy of new discoveries to the deep satisfaction of preserving pieces of history, making a profit, and remembering the friendships that blossom from shared interests.

Reflecting on my journey, I realize that coin collecting has enriched my life. It has been filled with constant learning, unexpected joys, and a deep connection to history. The friendships I've forged and the stories I've uncovered through each coin have been as valuable as the coins themselves.

For those of you who might feel overwhelmed as beginners, take heart, as every expert collector was once a beginner. Your journey in coin collecting is bound to be as rewarding as it is enriching. Take it one step at a time, and remember, the numismatic community is here to support you.

For further exploration, I recommend consulting resources such as the American Numismatic Association website, Coin World magazine, and various online numismatic forums and databases. These can offer ongoing support and updated information to help you grow and thrive in your collecting endeavors.

Your future in coin collecting is a tapestry of opportunities. You will build valuable collections, make savvy investments, and enjoy a fulfilling hobby that ties you to a community of passionate collectors and the rich world of numismatics.

Welcome to the world of coin collecting, a journey that promises endless learning and innumerable joys. Now is the time to collect, connect, and cherish. Happy collecting!

References

- Corporate Finance Institute. (n.d.). Numismatics - Overview, history, in the modern world. Retrieved from https://corporatefinanceinstitute.com/resources/wealth-management/numismatics

- NGC. (n.d.). NGC coin grading scale. Retrieved from https://www.ngccoin.com/coin-grading/grading-scale/

- GoldBroker. (n.d.). Bullion vs numismatic coins. Retrieved from https://goldbroker.com/investing-guide/bullion-vs-numismatics-coins#:~:text=There%20are%20two%20types%20of,often%20sought%20for%20their%20rarity.

- The Spruce Crafts. (n.d.). Coin collecting supplies for the beginner. Retrieved from https://www.thesprucecrafts.com/coin-collecting-supplies-for-the-beginner-768294

- Wikipedia. (n.d.). Mint mark. Retrieved from https://en.wikipedia.org/wiki/Mint_mark#:~:text=The%20current%20mint%20marks%20on,9%20official%20United%20States%20Mints.

- XAU. (n.d.). Circulated vs. uncirculated coins: What's the difference and ... Retrieved from https://xau.ca/circulated-vs-uncirculated-coins-mint-coins/#:~:text=Circulated%20coins%20have%20been%20used,are%20thus%20in%20pristine%20condition.

- NGC. (n.d.). Silver commemoratives (1892-1954) | Price guide & values. Retrieved from https://www.ngccoin.com/price-guide/united-states/commemoratives/71/

- Investopedia. (n.d.). Bullion coins: What they are, how they work, example. Retrieved from https://www.investopedia.com/terms/b/bullion-coins.asp

- Physical Gold. (n.d.). 8 proven techniques to check if a coin is counterfeit. Retrieved from https://www.physicalgold.com/insights/techniques-to-check-if-a-coin-is-counterfeit

- American Numismatic Association. (n.d.). 10 invaluable tips for purchasing collectible coins online. Retrieved from https://blog.money.org/coin-collecting/online-coin-buying-tips

- CoinWeek. (n.d.). Jeff Garrett: Great stories make coins great. Retrieved from https://coinweek.com/jeff-garrett-great-stories-make-coins-great/

- OpenNumismat. (n.d.). OpenNumismat - free coin collecting software. Retrieved from http://opennumismat.github.io/

- PCGS. (n.d.). Coin collecting tools on the go: PCGS mobile apps. Retrieved from https://www.pcgs.com/apps

- The Spruce Crafts. (n.d.). Protecting, preserving and storing your coin collection. Retrieved from https://www.thesprucecrafts.com/protecting-and-storing-coin-collections-768326

- BCW Supplies. (n.d.). What coin storage method is best for your coin collection? Retrieved from https://www.bcwsupplies.com/blog/2020/12/22/best-coin-storage-method/

- Sullivan Numismatics. (n.d.). Mint error definitions. Retrieved from https://sullivannumismatics.com/mint-error-definitions/

- PCGS. (n.d.). PCGS grading standards. Retrieved from https://www.pcgs.com/grades

- Focus on the User. (n.d.). PCGS reviews & complaints: Scam or reputable? Retrieved from https://www.focuson

theuser.org/dealers/pcgs.com-reviews/

- Physical Gold. (n.d.). 8 proven techniques to check if a coin is counterfeit. Retrieved from https://www.physicalgold.com/insights/techniques-to-check-if-a-coin-is-counterfeit

- Preservation Equipment. (n.d.). How to store coins - full guide. Retrieved from https://www.preservationequipment.com/Blog/Blog-Posts/How-to-store-coins-full-guide#:~:text=Storing%20coins%20in%20a%20box&text=Storing%20your%20coins%20in%20an,and%20painted%20surfaces%20like%20enamel.

- Zerust. (n.d.). Preventing silver coin tarnish an imperative to collectors. Retrieved from https://www.zerustproducts.com/anti-tarnish/preventing-silver-coin-tarnish-an-imperative-to-collectors/

- Publish What You Pay. (n.d.). Care and preservation of your numismatic coin collection. Retrieved from https://www.publishwhatyoupay.org/care-and-preservation-of-your-numismatic-coin-collection/#:~:text=Exposure%20to%20air%2C%20moisture%2C%20and,in%20airtight%20containers%20with%20desiccants.

- Coin Community. (n.d.). Has anyone used ANACS conservation service? Retrieved from https://www.coincommunity.com/forum/topic.asp?TOPIC_ID=435777

- APMEX. (n.d.). The role of coins in history. Retrieved from https://learn.apmex.com/learning-guide/history/the-role-of-coins-in-history/

- American Mint. (n.d.). Guide to commemorative coins. Retrieved from https://www.americanmint.com/commemorative-coins-guide

- CoinWeek. (n.d.). A guide to ancient coin collecting. Retrieved from https://coinweek.com/a-guide-to-ancient-coin-collecting/

- Forum Ancient Coins. (n.d.). Ancient coin authentication 101. Retrieved from https://www.forumancientcoins.com/NumisWiki/view.asp?key=Ancient%20Coin%20Authentication%20101

- PCGS. (n.d.). Coin market remains vibrant heading into 2023. Retrieved from https://www.pcgs.com/news/coin-market-remains-vibrant-heading-into-2023

- Płoński, P. (n.d.). Undervalued tokens — how to find them? Retrieved from https://medium.com/@MLJARofficial/undervalued-tokens-how-to-find-them-f4d80b399479

- Investopedia. (n.d.). How collectibles are taxed. Retrieved from https://www.investopedia.com/articles/personal-finance/061715/how-are-collectibles-taxed.asp

- The Royal Mint. (n.d.). Investing in historic coins. Retrieved from https://www.royalmint.com/stories/collect/investing-in-historic-coins/

- Collect Insure. (2023, July 6). Psychology of collecting: Why do people collect things? Retrieved from https://collectinsure.com/2023/07/06/psychology-of-collecting-why-do-people-collect-things/

- Rajesh, G. (n.d.). The history and significance of rare coins and currency. Retrieved from https://medium.com/@gkexamsrajesh/the-history-and-significance-of-rare-coins-and-currency-4f2bdf0de2ff

- Rocky Mountain Coin. (n.d.). Ways to curate your currency collection. Retrieved from https://rmcoin.com/blog/currency-collecting-blog/5-themed-ways-to-curate-your-currency-collection/

- International Coin Collectors. (n.d.). Coin collectors preserve history for future generations. Retrieved from https://iccoin.com/blog/coin-collectors-preserve-history-for-future-generations/

- Bottom Line Inc. (n.d.). Why you should join a coin-collecting club (and the best ...). Retrieved from https://www.bottomlineinc.com/blogs/money-connoisseur/best-coin-collecting-clubs

- Crypto.com. (n.d.). Avoiding digital currency scams. Retrieved from https://help.crypto.com/en/articles/6484926-avoiding-digital-currency-scams

- American Numismatic Society. (n.d.). American Numismatic Society: Home. Retrieved from https://numismatics.org/

- American Numismatic Association. (n.d.). Numismatic community. Retrieved from https://www.money.org/community/

- Physical Gold. (n.d.). 8 proven techniques to check if a coin is counterfeit. Retrieved from https://www.physicalgold.com/insights/techniques-to-check-if-a-coin-is-counterfeit

- Coinage Magazine. (n.d.). 15 tips to safely buy coins online. Retrieved from https://www.coinagemag.com/15-tips-to-safely-buy-coins-online/

- NGC. (n.d.). The difference between "cleaning" and "conservation ... Retrieved from https://boards.ngccoin.com/topic/71797-what-you-need-to-know-the-difference-between-cleaning-and-conservation/

- The Motley Fool. (n.d.). Investors lose over $100 million in silver coin scam. How ... Retrieved from https://www.fool.com/the-ascent/buying-stocks/articles/investors-lose-over-100-million-in-silver-coin-scam-how-to-buy-gold-and-silver-safely/

- ACC Guild. (2021, April 7). US import restrictions on ancient coins (current as of April ...). Retrieved from https://accguild.org/resources/Documents/Import%20Restrictions%

- Liberty Coin & Currency. (n.d.). Five ways to spot a fake coin. Retrieved from https://libertycoinandcurrency.com

/blog/five-ways-to-spot-a-fake-coin/

- Professional Numismatists Guild. (n.d.). PNG code of ethics. Retrieved from https://www.pngdealers.org/ethics#:~:text=To%20refrain%20from%20knowingly%20participating,making%20any%20attempt%20to%20deceive.

- CoinTalk. (n.d.). Success stories in coin collecting. Retrieved from https://www.cointalk.com/threads/success-stories-in-coin-collecting.285701/

- APMEX. (n.d.). A beginner's guide to error coins. Retrieved from https://learn.apmex.com/learning-guide/numismatics/beginners-guide-to-error-coins/

- Britannica. (n.d.). Coin collecting: History, value & types. Retrieved from https://www.britannica.com/topic/coin-collecting

- Blanchard Gold. (n.d.). How to get started in collecting rare coins on a budget. Retrieved from https://www.blanchardgold.com/market-news/how-to-get-started-in-collecting-rare-coins-on-a-budget/#:~:text=Prioritizing%20quality%20over%20quantity%20is,them%20more%20desirable%20among%20collectors.

- American Numismatic Association. (n.d.). World's Fair of Money®. Retrieved from https://www.money.org/worldsfairofmoney/

- FOX40. (n.d.). Coin apps to help you identify the change in your pocket. Retrieved from https://fox40.com/news/national-and-world-news/want-to-change-your-fortune-coin-apps-might-help/#:~:text=CoinFacts%20(PCGS%20mobile%20app)%26text=PCGS%20claims%20they're%20the,and%20value%20of%20different%20coins.

- American Numismatic Society. (n.d.). Online resources. Retrieved from https://numismatics.org/resources/

- PCMag. (n.d.). Take these 5 steps to stop apps from collecting your data now. Retrieved from https://www.pcmag.com/how-to/take-these-steps-to-stop-apps-from-collecting-your-data-now

- Numismatic News. (n.d.). Online forums a good resource for collectors. Retrieved from https://www.numismaticnews.net/collecting-101/online-forums-a-good-resource-for-collectors

- Blanchard Gold. (n.d.). The world's 8 largest and most famous coin hoards. Retrieved from https://www.blanchardgold.com/market-news/famous-coin-hoards/#:~:text=One%20notable%20discovery%20is%20the,hoards%20ever%20unearthed%20in%20Britain.

- Blanchard Gold. (n.d.). Shipwreck coins and bars. Retrieved from https://www.blanchardgold.com/guide/shipwreck/

- ScienceDirect. (n.d.). Ancient coin designs encoded increasing amounts of information. Retrieved from https://www.sciencedirect.com/science/article/pii/S0278416519300315

- Finest Known. (n.d.). Great collectors, great collections. Retrieved from https://finestknown.com/1782-2/

- Investor Ideas. (2022, June 17). How to choose a theme for your coin collection. Retrieved from https://www.investorideas.com/news/2022/mining/06172Theme-For-Coin-Collection.asp

- Street Directory. (n.d.). 7 most common coin collecting themes. Retrieved from https://www.streetdirectory.com/etoday/7-most-common-coin-collecting-themes-elujwa.html

- Liberty Street Software. (n.d.). CoinManage inventory & value your coin collection. Retrieved from https://www.libertystreet.com/Coin-Collecting-Software.htm

- Invaluable. (n.d.). How to store and display a coin collection. Retrieved from https://www.invaluable.com/blog/t

he-best-ways-to-display-your-coin-collection/

- Physical Gold. (n.d.). 8 proven techniques to check if a coin is counterfeit. Retrieved from https://www.physicalgold.com/insights/techniques-to-check-if-a-coin-is-counterfeit

- CoinWeek. (n.d.). Budget coin collecting: How to raise money to buy better coins. Retrieved from https://coinweek.com/budget-coin-collecting-how-to-raise-money-to-buy-better-coins/

- Preservation Equipment. (n.d.). How to store coins - full guide. Retrieved from https://www.preservationequipment.com/Blog/Blog-Posts/How-to-store-coins-full-guide

- APMEX. (n.d.). Insurance: How to insure a coin collection. Retrieved from https://learn.apmex.com/learning-guide/coin-collecting/how-to-insure-a-coin-collection/

- LoveToKnow. (n.d.). Coin collection appraisal tips to recognize their true value. Retrieved from https://www.lovetoknow.com/home/antiques-collectibles/coin-collectors-appraisal

- U.S. Mint. (n.d.). Caring for your coin collection. Retrieved from https://www.usmint.gov/learn/collecting-basics/caring-for-your-coin-collection

- Precious Metals. (n.d.). Guide to passing down your coin collection to heirs. Retrieved from https://www.preciousmetals.com/blog/post/passing-down-your-coin-collection.htm

- Wikipedia. (n.d.). Sheldon coin grading scale. Retrieved from https://en.wikipedia.org/wiki/Sheldon_coin_grading_scale

- PCGS. (n.d.). The tools of a professional coin grader. Retrieved from https://www.pcgs.com/news/tools-of-a-professional-coin-grader

- Coin Appraiser. (n.d.). Everything you need to know about

- coin grading. Retrieved from https://coinappraiser.com/pcgs-ngc-grading/

- Coin Imaging. (n.d.). Coin photography article. Retrieved from https://coinimaging.com/photography.html#:~:text=To%20do%20this%20you%20need,needs%20to%20be%20extra%20osteady.

- NGC. (n.d.). Jeff Garrett: Changing trends in numismatics. Retrieved from https://www.ngccoin.com/news/article/11171/

- Satta Blog Post King. (n.d.). The impact of blockchain technology on authenticating rare coins. Retrieved from https://sattablogpostking.com.in/?p=738

- Toolify. (n.d.). The future of coin grading: AI revolutionizes the market. Retrieved from https://www.toolify.ai/ai-news/the-future-of-coin-grading-ai-revolutionizes-the-market-2475668

- GovMint. (n.d.). The 9 best coin resources for collectors online. Retrieved from https://www.govmint.com/coin-authority/post/the-best-coin-resources-for-collectors-online

- Numismatic News. (n.d.). The Sheldon coin grading scale. Retrieved from https://www.numismaticnews.net/collecting-101/the-sheldon-coin-grading-scale

- Wikipedia. (n.d.). Sheldon coin grading scale. Retrieved from https://en.wikipedia.org/wiki/Sheldon_coin_grading_scale